Shirley Temple

Identification and
Price Guide to
Shirley Temple
Collectibles

by Suzanne Kraus-Mancuso

Hobby House Press

Published by
Hobby House Press, Inc.
Grantsville, Maryland
www.hobbyhouse.com

Dedication

For Dorothy Kraus, Minnie Williams, Lorraine Hoffman
& Baby Steven—I wish you were here!
For Joseph, Katie, Jamie & Justin, Mother and Dad
I Love You All!

Additional copies of this book may be purchased at $24.95
(plus postage and handling) from
Hobby House Press, Inc.
1 Corporate Drive, Grantsville, MD 21536
1-800-554-1447
www.hobbyhouse.com
or from your favorite bookstore or dealer.

©2002 by Suzanne Mancuso

Printed in the United States of America

ISBN: 0-87588-624-8

Acknowledgements

I would like to thank the following people and organizations for their generous contributions towards the making of this book: Rita Dubas, Loretta McKenzie, Loretta Beilstein, Tonya Bevardi, James Walski, Bernice Arborlay, Arline Roth, Nancy Shamberger, Lorraine Burdick, Patricia Smith, Jackie Musgrave, Donna Carr, Bonnie Braun, Billie Nelson-Tyrell, Pat Vaillancourt, Judith Izen, Marge Meisinger, Mary Strucher, Monica Sudds, Cathy Kaufman, Cathy Grey, Lorraine Hoffman, Dorothy Kraus, Sabrina Kraus, Maxine & William Kraus, Bill Jordan, Ardis Danon, Carol Birney, Linda Keiderer, Ben and Mary Mancuso, Eleanor McBride, Mary Florenz, Ursula Schink, Mary Ann Schunk, Nancy Augustowski, Adele Hobby, Kathy Zimmerman, Alice Maffia, Joan and Richard Kaaihue, Vandy Weihn, Doris Parker, Sharon Geurtin, John Perfetti, The Sleepy Hollow Doll Club, United Federation of Doll Clubs (U.F.D.C.), The Shirley Temple Collectors by the Sea, Dover Publications, Shirley Temple Collectors News and The Yorktown Museum.

Photography and technical support provided by: Whitney Lane Photographers, Ken & Susan Quarato, Louis Metcalf, Joseph A Mancuso, Rankin Bettcher, Joan F. Mancuso, J.W Townson.

Collages provided by William F. Kraus.

1934 Original large postcard
$15

Table of Contents

6   Preface

Chapter 1
8   A Girl Named Shirley Jane
10 History & Movie Chronology

Chapter 2
18 A Step In Shirley's Time
    1930's Fashions, Paper & Miscellaneous Items

Chapter 3
38 The Composition Doll

Chapter 4
72 The Vinyl Dolls From the 50's, 60's, 70's & 80's

Chapter 5
108 You Name It, They Made It!

Chapter 6
132 Restoration and Care

Chapter 7
138 The Shirley Connection

Chapter 8
142 Resources

Chapter 9
148 Shirley Temple Facts and Fun

Prologue
152 "The Slab Story"

158 Index

160 About the Author

Preface

The word "fan" is derived from the word "fanatic". There are fans of all types in the world. Some fanatics collect sports stuff. Others collect stamps. Then there's me. I collect (hoard) as much Shirley Temple memorabilia as I can. I scour flea markets and antique shops, searching for that new (old) Shirley doll or photo. And race it back home to add to the collection.

The veteran fans were the children (and adults) of the 1930's. These were the people from the depression era. They saw the original movies in black and white, purchased the dolls and many collectibles for less than a buck, and grew up begging their mothers to curl their hair and send them to tap lessons. They lived through the actual "Shirley Temple Craze".

The next generation of fans grew from the popular children's show in the 1950's. These Children watched the *Shirley Temple Story Hour* on TV, and were able to hear the fabled stories from their mothers about this talented youngster in her early years. This created a renewed interest in Shirley, and more collectibles were released to the public to satisfy the needs of the younger generation.

The third generation of fans (this is where I fall) came from the regained popularity of Shirley dolls in the 1970's. My grandmother purchased the 1972 vinyl version of *Stand Up & Cheer* for me when I was six years old. I have been hooked ever since! My generation has to pay top dollar for the "antique" dolls, and we have to fight over them on eBay™ as well.

The forth version of fans are the children of the new millennium. My children, who see colorized versions of Shirley Temple movies on TV, who will see *The Life of Shirley Temple Child Star, The Shirley Temple Story* on TV, and can obtain new Shirley dolls from Danbury Mint.

To date, there are still many items being manufactured in the likeness of Shirley Temple. Even sixty some odd years later, there is still a demand for her dolls and collectibles. In the future, I see the "fans" carrying on the love and need for Shirley Temple items. I also hope the desire to collect Shirley Temple memorabilia carries on for many years to come. My message to them is clear, "Carry on, fellow Shirley fans, carry on!"

Still America's Sweetheart collage.
Designed by William F. Kraus.

Colorized promotional photo of Shirley holding her *Little Dutch Dolly*.
(Joan Kaaihue)

Shirley Temple, photo taken from the film *Wee Willie Winkie*.
$3-$5

Chapter 1

A Girl Named Shirley Jane

On April 23, 1928, a baby girl was born in Santa Monica California. Her given name was Shirley Jane Temple. I often wonder if George and Gertrude Temple really ever knew the magnitude of the impact that their daughter would have on the world.

Shirley Temple began her career in show business at the tender age of three, and has stayed in the public's eye ever since. Shirley was given the amazing talents of singing, dancing and cheering people that grew into a political career that spanned over six decades. Over the course of those sixty years, Shirley Temple has traveled around the world gaining popularity in more ways than one. Shirley was always the picture of a childhood dream for the youngsters, and the epitome of a Hollywood legend as she grew into the political person she became.

It has been previously stated that once Shirley reached adolescence, her popularity diminished due to that one thing Hollywood can't control, her age. But in my research, Shirley Temple is the one actress in the world that has made it to the top and remained there. Unlike many of her co-stars and friends, Shirley has managed to survive the Hollywood lion and live to tell about it. She never fell pray to the many dangers of stardom, and she never succumbed to the multitude of elements that has claimed the lives of so many other famous people.

Shirley Temple is extremely popular today with a whole new audience to entertain; however, it is very hard to explain to these young fans that the cute little girl dancing on the TV is a mother and a grandmother now, and that she had a very busy life between tapping in *Stand Up & Cheer* to assisting with several Presidential issues, not to mention the many other humanitarian deeds that she has accomplished in her lifetime. As you can see, Shirley Temple has accomplished great triumphs in her time, and she still continues to hold her audiences and fans.

Shirley Temple, photo taken from the film *Captain January* along with the cast Guy Kibbee and Slim Summerville.
$3-$5

Shirley Temple's History & Movie Chronology

1928
- April 23, Shirley Jane Temple was born

1931
- Meglins Dance School Begins, Shirley gets discovered

1932
- A Series of Short Films Were Made
  War Babies
  The Runt Page
  Pie Covered Wagon
  Glad Rags to Riches

1933
  The Red Haired Alibi
  Kid 'n' Hollywood
  Polly-Tix in Washington
  Kid 'n' Africa
  Merrily Yours
  Dora's Dunkin Donuts
  The Kids Last Fight
  To The Last Man
  Out All Night

1934
- February, Shirley Temple signs Fox Films contract
- Shirley receives a miniature Oscar from Academy Awards
  Pardon My Pups
  Managed Money
  New Deal Rhythm
  Carolina
  Mandalay
  Now I'll Tell
  Change Of Heart
  Stand Up & Cheer
  Little Miss Marker
  Baby, Take a Bow
  Now and Forever
  Bright Eyes
- Ideal Toy Co. creates the Shirley Temple doll

1935
- February 27, Shirley Meets President Franklin D. Roosevelt
- Shirley Meets Amelia Earhardt
- Fox Studios and 20th Century Studio's merge making the studio 20th Century Fox™
- Studio creates "The Shirley Temple Film Development Division"
  The Little Colonel
  Our Little Girl
  Curly Top
  The Littlest Rebel
- Shirley leaves footprints at Graumann's Chinese Theatre

1936
  Captain January
  Poor Little Rich Girl
  Dimples
  Stowaway

1937
  Wee Willie Winkie
  Heidi
- Shirley leaves her footprints in concrete at Rhode's Theatre (Chicago)

1938
  Rebecca of Sunny Brook Farm

1939
  Just Around The Corner
  The Little Princess
  Susanna of the Mounties
  The Blue Bird

1940
- September, Shirley enters Westlake School for Girls
  Young People

1941
  Kathleen

1942
  Miss Annie Rooney
- Shirley's contract with 20th Century Fox ends

Shirley Temple, photo taken from the film *Captain January*
wearing her famous (yellow) raincoat.
$3-$5

1943
- Springtime, Shirley signs movie contract with Selznick International

1944
  Since You Went Away
  I'll Be Seeing You

1945
- Springtime, Shirley graduates from the Westlake school for Girls
  Kiss and Tell
- September 19, Shirley Temple marries John Agar
- Honeymoon
  The Bachelor and the Bobbysoxer

1947
  That Hagen Girl

1948
- January 30, birth of daughter Linda Susan
  Fort Apache

1949
- January 20, attends President Truman's Inauguration
  Adventures in Baltimore
  Mr. Belvedere Goes To Washington
  The Story of Sea Biscuit
  A Kiss For Corliss
- December 5, Shirley Temple divorces John Agar
- October, Shirley's contract with Selznick International ends

1950
- December 16, Shirley marries Mr. Charles Black
- May, Mr. And Mrs. Black moves to Maryland

1952
- April 28, birth of son Charles Alden Black, Jr.

1953
- June, Shirley visits President Dwight D. Eisenhower
- Shirley and Charles move to Los Angeles, California

1954
- April, birth of daughter Lori Alden Black
- Shirley stays out of the public eye for a short time

- Ideal makes a new series of vinyl dolls, and Fox re-releases Shirley's movies for TV
- The Black's move to Atherton, California

1958
- January 12, *Shirley Temple's Storybook* series airs on TV

1960
- September 18, *The Shirley Temple Show* series airs on TV
- Shirley campaigns for Richard Nixon's losing presidential race
- Shirley and Charles move to Woodside, California
- Shirley becomes the co-founder of the National Federation of Multiple Sclerosis Societies (Shirley's brother George is afflicted with MS)

1965
- San Francisco Health Facilities Planning Association (Shirley is a board member)
- Travels to Russia for International Federation of Multiple Sclerosis Societies (IFMSS)

1967
- Shirley runs in the California Congressional campaign

1968
- Shirley Temple Black is awarded Dame, Order of Knights of Malta, Paris
- Shirley travels to Prague for IFMSS
- Campaigns for Richard Nixon

1969
- Shirley Temple Black is appointed Director to the Bank of California
- Director, Fireman's Fund Insurance Company
- Director, BANCAL Tri-State Corporation
- Director, Del Monte Corporation
- Member, California Advisory Hospital Council

1969-70
Representative to 24th General Assembly of United Nations (appointed by Richard Nixon)

1972-74
- Special assistant to chairman, American Council on Environmental Quality

Promotional photo that would have been given away with a Shirley Temple doll.
Shirley is holding a doll in a matching striped dress.
$8-$10
(Eleanor McBride)

1972
- Shirley becomes a representative, UN Conference on Human Environment To Stockholm (appointed by William Rogers)
- Delegate treaty on environment U.S.S.R.-U.S.A. Joint Committee, Moscow
- Shirley has breast cancer (undergoes mastectomy)
- Ideal releases a new vinyl Shirley Temple doll series

1972
- Member U.S. Commission for UNESCO

1974
- May 28, Shirley is "elected" as Director, Walt Disney Productions

1974-76
- Ambassador to Ghana (appointed by President Gerald R. Ford)

1975
- October 8, Marriage of Linda Susan to Robert Falaschi

1976-77
- Shirley becomes U.S. Chief of Protocol (appointed by President Gerald R. Ford)
- Shirley is in charge of arrangements for inauguration and inaugural ball for President Jimmy Carter

1977
- January 1, Shirley's mother, Gertrude Temple, dies
- Shirley receives the Life Achievement Award of the American Center For Children

1980
- September 30, Shirley's father, George Temple, dies
- December 20, birth of granddaughter, Theresa Lyn Falaschi

1981
- Shirley becomes a member to the U.S. Delegation on African Refugee Problems in Geneva

- Appointed to Board of Directors, National Wildlife Federation
- Member, UN Association, United States Founding Member, American Academy of Diploma Chairman, Ambassadorial Seminars

1982
- To the present, Danbury Mint produces "new" bisque collector's dolls
- Named new President of the Commonwealth Club of California

1985
- Shirley was presented with a full-sized Oscar
- Publishes her autobiography *Child Star: An Autobiography*

1989
- Shirley Temple Black is Grand Marshal for Rose Bowl Parade for the second time

1999
- Shirley Appears in *People Magazine* "Where Are They Now?"

2000
- Shirley's 50th Wedding Anniversary to Charles Black

2001
- Made for TV movie *The Shirley Temple Story* based on the book *Child Star: An Autobiography* written by Shirley Temple Black, directed by Paula and Melissa Joan Hart and starring Ashley Rose Orr.
- Presently, Shirley Temple Black lives in California with her husband Charles. She has been working on her second book (considered the follow up to her book *Child Star: An Autobiography* published in 1988)
- In the past, Shirley Temple Black would read and respond to her multitude of fan mail and autograph requests. However, due to the posting of her name and address on the Internet, the number of people requesting her autograph has skyrocketed to the point that Shirley has to return MOST of the mail to the senders.

Vintage photo giveaway.
$8-$10

Chapter 2

A Step in Shirley's Time

1930's Fashions, Paper & Miscellaneous Items

Back in the 1930's, there was no such thing as TV or Nintendo. Most children listened to radio programs and went to the movies if they could afford a ticket. Shirley Temple just so happened to be box office queen from 1935-1939; the advertisers and toy companies took full advantage of this. Nearly every little girl in the world wanted to look like Shirley Temple, and have her many dresses and fashionable accessories. Shirley Temple was a definite trendsetter and fashion icon for the children of this period

Above:
Green child's purse with duck appliqué with small hand held mirror.
$125
(Rita Dubas)

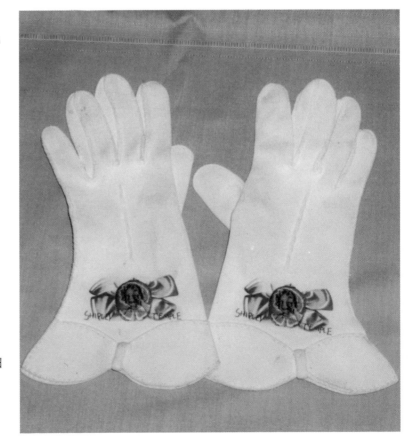

Right:
White gloves with Shirley Temple photo and blue ribbon imprinted on them.
$65
(Donna Carr)

New printed cotton
T-shirt with *Wee Willie Winkie*
taken from an old movie poster.
$35
(Donna Carr)

Brown leather shoes. Bottom reads "The
Authentic Shirley Temple Shoe" Made by
the James McCreey Co., New York.
$75
(Loretta Beilstein)

13in x 10in (33cm x 25cm) Unusual 3-D plaster photo from the 1930's.
This picture of Shirley is adhered to a plaster base, which is molded to conform
to the black and white portrait giving it a 3-dimentional effect.
This medium was very common during this era.
$250-$300
(Rita Dubas)

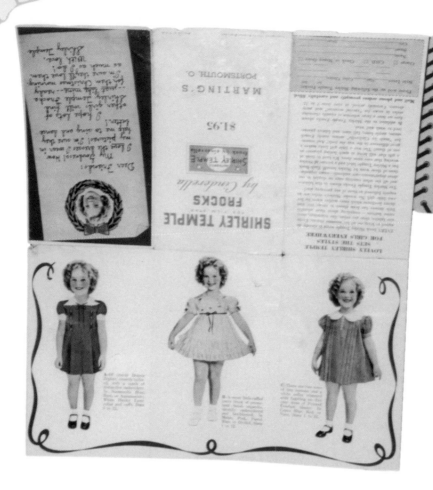

1930's Brochure for Cinderella dresses; label reads "Shirley Temple Frocks".
$45
(Loretta Beilstein)

Box cover for Authentic Shirley Temple bathing suits by Forest Mills.
$75-$100
(Rita Dubas)

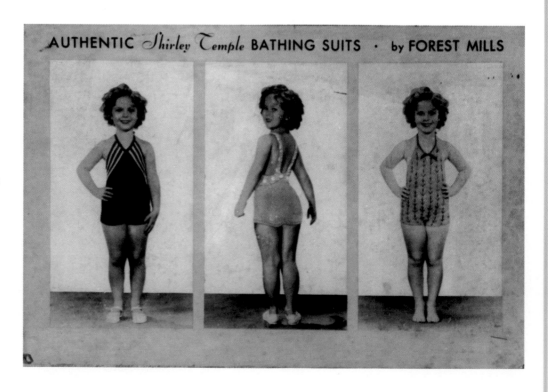

1936 Shirley Temple movie poster from the film *Dimples*.
$1800
(Rita Dubas)

Shirley Temple Glamour Girl
Beauty Set by Starburst.
$75
(Donna Carr)

Shirley Temple Hair Styler
#339 by Starburst.
$75
(Donna Carr)

Ideal Dolly Make-up Kit for a
Shirley Temple doll.
$150
(Loretta Beilstein)

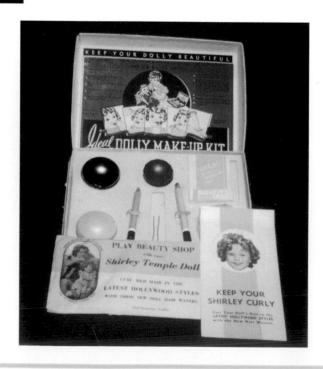

Above:
Shirley Temple hair bow and band on it's original package.
$45
(James Walski)

Right:
1959. Original Shirley Temple clothes ad. *McCall's.*

A rollicking crew of salty separates. Flag-white shirt in sizes 3 to 6x, about $1.50 and 7 to 14, about $2.00. Navy shorts appliqued in white, sizes 3 to 6x, and 7 to 14, about $2.00. Jamaica shorts in sizes 7 to 14, about $2.50. Slim Jims in sizes 3 to 6x, about $2.50 and 7 to 14, about $3.00. For store nearest you, write Rosenau Brothers, Inc., Fox St. & Roberts Ave., Phila. 29, Pa.

Above:
Original 22in x 15in (56cm x 38cm)
Store posters from 1935. This was a
store display for Cinderella Frocks.
$65-$85
(Loretta Beilstein)

Left:
Shirley Temple Fox Star, photo of Shirley
(Rita Dubas)

A Shirley Temple paper doll standing cutout, measures 4¾ in (10cm), made by W.J. Caley & Co. Inc. Novelty from Vassar Weavers Hair Accessories.
$25-$35
(Loretta Beilstein)

A very rare authentic 1930's salesman's briefcase featuring two photos—one of Shirley standing next to a table, the other of a Shirley "look-a-like".
$500
(Rita Dubas)

Original 1930's ad for *Bringing up Shirley* by Gertrude Temple, *The American Magazine.*
$75
(Rita Dubas)

Real $1 bill with a Shirley decal sticker over George Washington's face. Sold as a novelty, these came with many different stickers of Shirley pictured.
$3 to $5.

1984 Indian Headband Souvenir reads Shirley Temple for President.
$45
(Donna Carr)

An original Fox catalog, 23 selling aids manufactured by Fox Film Corporation for retail merchants. Contains: Buttons, window stand ups, booklets, cutouts, hangers, 40in x 60in (102cm x 152cm) blow-ups, window displays, photos, clothes, cards and posters. Very rare and hard to find.
$400
(Loretta Beilstein)

Shirley Temple paper dolls on the left, boxed paper dolls with movie costumes from 1976.
$ 25-$35
On the right:
Classic Shirley Temple paper dolls in full color, published by Dover and are still available, issue price
$4.95

Stand-up Shirley Temple paper dolls featured
life-like hair 1958 by the Gabriel Company.
$75
(Loretta Beilstein)

Close-up of 1935 Shirley
Temple paper dolls in
springtime outfits.
$20
(Kathy Zimmerman)

Authentic Shirley Temple Black
autograph, signed at her 1995
book signing tour for her book
Child Star: An Autobiography.
$75

Shirley Temple Black 1995
autographed photo on marble plaque.
$225

1935 Original 17in x 36in
(43cm x 91cm)
cardboard movie poster for
the film *The Little Colonel.*
$100
(Loretta Beilstein)

1945 27in x 41in (69cm x 104cm)
Original paper movie poster for the film
Kiss and Tell.
$100
(Loretta Beilstein)

1947 Original cardboard poster,
22in x 28 in (56cm x 71cm)
for the film *That Hagen Girl.*
$100
(Loretta Beilstein)

Shirley Temple promotional cardboard cutout
for a necklace with holes punched through for
necklace to appear.
$75
(Rita Dubas)

Above:
1949 14in x 36in (36cm x 91cm) Original
cardboard poster *Mr. Belvedere Goes to College*.
$100
(Loretta Beilstein)

Right:
1930's 13in x 16in (33cm x 41cm)
Star hangers sold by Fox Exchange for
10¢ each, printed on both sides.
$55
(Loretta Beilstein)

1935 Original *Miss America* movie poster.
$1800
(Rita Dubas)

1935 Movie poster from France
for the film *The Littlest Rebel*
(Shadow of Lionel Barrymore).
$1800
(Rita Dubas)

1936 Movie poster from France
for the film *Captain January*.
$1800
(Rita Dubas)

1936 Movie poster *Stowaway*.
$1800
(Rita Dubas)

1936 Foreign *Stowaway*
poster.
$1800
(Rita Dubas)

1958 *TV Guide*. Shirley Temple: Twenty Years After

ITEMS NOT SHOWN

Shirley Temple song sheets/sheet music
Good condition $15-$20 and up
Poor condition (Faded, ripped, marked on, or bent) $5-$7

Shirley Temple song albums
Good condition $15- $20
Poor condition $5-$7

Shirley Temple coloring book pre-1940, $25-$35

Shirley Temple 11in x14in (28cm x 36cm) magazine movie posters pullouts from 1930's $35-$45, pullouts from the 1940's $25-$35.

Shirley Temple cigar bands (domestic and foreign) $15-$20 and up

Shirley Temple giveaway photos $8-$10

Shirley Temple scrapbooks $12-$15
1930's Shirley Temple postcards
Domestic $15, Foreign $20 and up

1930's Tobacco cards
Domestic $15, Foreign $20 each
Complete sets $125 and up

1930's Shirley Temple dress tags for Nannette, Cinderella, dresses, frocks, shoes and socks $15-$35 for tags in excellent condition.

Original Shirley Dress tags/NRA woven tags $8-$10

Shirley Temple magazine covers, magazine ads, photographs or pullouts
    Average items begin at $8-$10, rare items $15-$20 or more

Chapter 3

The Composition Doll

The Ideal Toy Company eventually made 9 different Shirley Temple dolls sizes, each of which came in an original dress or movie costume. The dolls were packaged with a giveaway photo and round pin-back pin. Included on the dolls were light pink underwear/slips trimmed with lace and white rayon socks with black or white leatherette buckle shoes. Sculpted by master doll artist Bernard Lipfert, he created a wax prototype of Shirley's face to achieve a doll in her likeness. The movie costumes were mass-produced by the "Mollye" clothing company, and were designed by Mollye Goldman. Her company exclusively designed these dresses from 1934 thru 1936 .

The dolls came in seven different sizes: 11in (28cm), 13in (33cm), 15-16in (38cm-41cm), 18 in (46cm), 20-22in (51-56cm), 25in (64cm) and 27in (69cm). The molds were changed slightly throughout the production of these dolls, which explains the different facial expressions and change in hairstyles.

Composition dolls were generally marked on the neck and upper back/torso of the doll. Some of the early prototypes had Ideal markings or SHIRLEY TEMPLE on the head and neck. Most of the later dolls were clearly marked on the head, neck or upper back with the SHIRLEY TEMPLE logo and doll's size printed on it.

These are some of the possible marks that may be found on the back of your dolls:

1. On the neck: SHIRLEY TEMPLE
   On the back: SHIRLEY TEMPLE
   13 (this number would reflect the doll's correct height)

2. On the neck: C-OP Ideal Toy Co. N&T (This stood for The Ideal Toy & Novelty Company)
   On the back: Shirley Temple

3. On the neck: (Ideal in a diamond-shape logo)

4. On the neck: Ideal Shirley Temple in a half-circle shape
   On the back: IDEAL

WITH LOVE....
SHIRLEY TEMPLE

22 in (56cm) Wigged baby Ideal Shirley Temple doll, shown in a large, deluxe Shirley Temple baby carriage made by the J.C. Whitney Company in 1935. The set came with an embroidered woolen blanket marked "Shirley Temple" on it along with an appliquéd lamb and fringe. All-original. When it was new, this set was sold for $9.95.
Doll/Carriage/Blanket set $4000
(Rita Dubas)

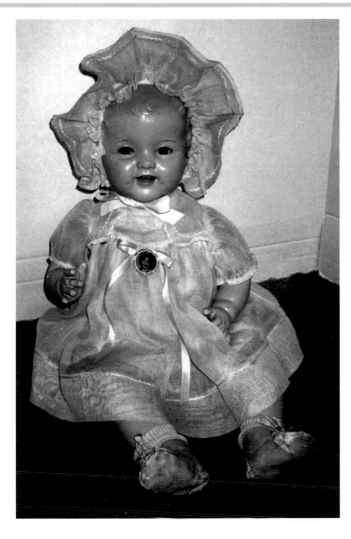

20in (51cm) Ideal baby Shirley Temple doll,
all-original with molded painted hair.
Composition head, hands and feet, cloth body.
Marked SHIRLEY TEMPLE IDEAL
$1000-$1200
(Tonya Bevardi)

Smaller sized composition Baby Shirley Doll
riding in an authentic Shirley Buggy.
Doll $700, Buggy $750 and up
(J. Mancuso)

13in (33cm) Ideal Shirley Temple composition doll wearing an original blue star pattern dress with lace collar. Original shoes and socks, replaced pin. From the film *Poor Little Rich Girl* marked IDEAL SHIRLEY TEMPLE 13.
$800

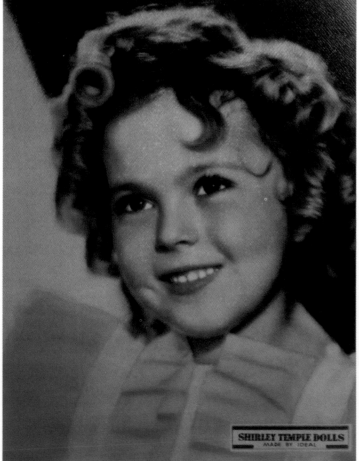

Original box cover for genuine Shirley Temple dolls.
$300
(Rita Dubas)

Original box cover for genuine
Shirley Temple doll clothes.
$300
(Rita Dubas)

Original box cover for authentic Shirley
Temple wardrobe trunk with doll.
$300
(Rita Dubas)

1935 13in (33cm) Ideal Shirley Temple
composition doll in the original box
wearing a tagged blue knife-pleated
cotton organdy dress. Marked on head:
Shirley Temple IDEAL 15
Original shoes, socks, and pin.
$1200
(Loretta Beilstein)

1936 20in (51cm) Ideal Shirley Temple
composition doll wearing a rare dress from
the movie *Poor Little Rich Girl*. Powder
blue "bow pattern" all-original with pin.
$1200-$1400
(Richard and Joan Kaaihue)

1935 18in (46cm) Ideal Shirley Temple composition doll wearing a rare sailboat dress from the film *Now I'll Tell* (includes original box, not shown).
$1200-$1300
(Richard and Joan Kaaihue)

20 in (51cm) Ideal Shirley Temple doll composition doll wearing the rare "Bolero" outfit. Note the darker, differently styled hair. This doll was one of Ideal's last advertised dolls before they were discontinued. All-original.
$1500
(Tonya Bevardi)

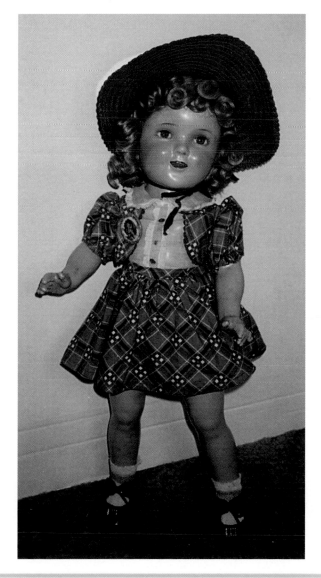

13in (33cm) Ideal Shirley Temple composition doll wearing tagged blue cotton organdy. Authentic trunk is complete with full wardrobe. All-original.
Doll/Dress $1500
Wardrobe trunk $500 and up
Original outfits $175-$250
(depending on rarity of dress)
Jumpsuits $150-$200
Original Shirley pin-back pins $150
(in good condition)
Original shoes and sock $125-$ 150
(Loretta McKenzie)

Slightly different version of Shirley doll with trunk wardrobe. All-original.
$1500
(Rita Dubas)

1934 13in (33cm) Ideal Shirley Temple composition doll wearing a yellow plaid dress from the film *Bright Eyes*. All-original.
Doll/Dress **$1100**
Fur Coat/Hat **$375**
(Joan Kaaihue)

1936 Ideal Shirley Temple composition doll wearing pink floral pattern dress from the film *Poor Little Rich Girl*. Make-up period doll with more grown up hairstyle.
$1500
(Richard and Joan Kaaihue)

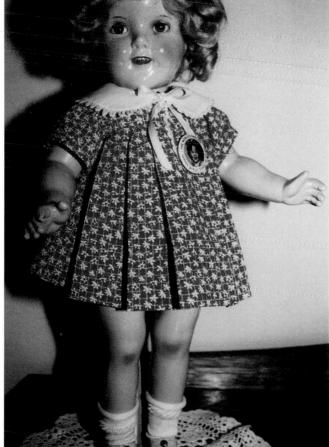

1934 18in (46cm) Ideal Shirley Temple
composition doll wearing a red dress with
striped trim from the film *Our Little Girl*.
The doll is marked with the early
C-op IDEAL logo.
$1500
(Tonya Bevardi)

1934 20in (51cm) Ideal Shirley Temple
composition doll wearing the blue version
of the dress from *Our Little Girl*.
$1200-$1300
(Loretta McKenzie)

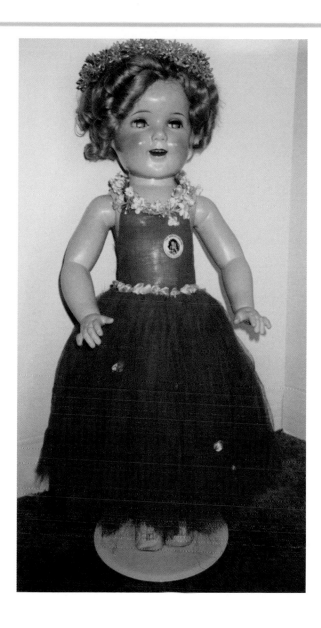

1939 27in (69cm) Ideal Shirley Temple composition doll wearing a pink full-length gown possibly from the dream sequence of the film *The Little Princess*. Unmarked dress, original pin, shoes and socks.
$2500
(Tonya Bevardi)

1934 13in (33cm) Ideal Shirley Temple composition doll wearing original dress from the film *Stand Up & Cheer*.
$1000-$1100
(Loretta McKenzie)

1934 15in (38cm) Ideal Shirley Temple composition doll wearing original pink organdy with a powder blue bow, lace collar and original shoes and socks. Replaced pin. Shoes have some damage. Marked on head with the early C-op IDEAL logo. **$800-$900**

Back view of doll's dress and tag marked Shirley Temple doll dress NPU.

Close up of a mint in-the-box, 1936 Ideal Shirley Temple composition doll. Common red and white dress from the film *Baby Take a Bow*.
$2000
(Loretta McKenzie)

Shirley Temple composition doll wearing a powder blue white dot swirl dress with rainbow trim. All-original and from the "make up" period.
$1500
(Loretta McKenzie)

1936 Ideal Shirley Temple composition doll wearing the "Canadian Reliable" green dress with matching tam from the film *Poor Little Rich Girl.*
$1200-$1400
(Loretta McKenzie)

1936 13in (33cm) Ideal Shirley Temple composition doll wearing a royal blue dress with a lace collar from the film *Poor Little Rich Girl.*
$1500
(Loretta McKenzie)

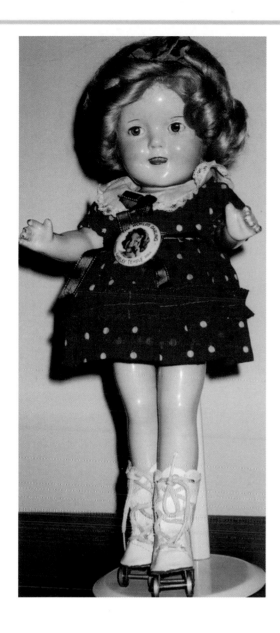

Ideal Shirley Temple composition doll wearing a red dress with white and blue dots from the film *The Littlest Rebel*. Roller skates are from a period "Sonja Hennie" doll.
$1200
(Loretta McKenzie)

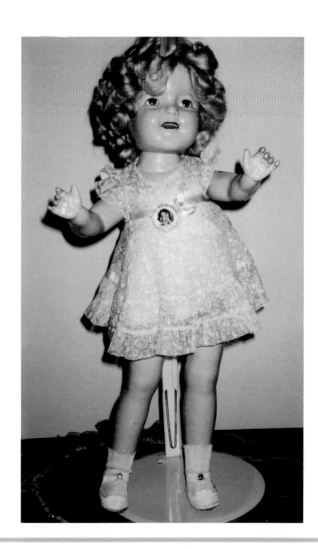

1934 22in (56cm) Ideal Shirley Temple composition doll wearing a rare floral version of "Dora's Dunking Donuts" dress.
$1700
(Loretta McKenzie)

28in (71cm) Rare tagged school dress from the film *Captain January*.
$1800-$2000
(Loretta McKenzie)

1936 16in (41cm) Ideal Shirley Temple composition doll wearing an original pink organdy dress with excellent facial coloring and a perfect wig set from the "make up" period.
$1400
(Loretta McKenzie)

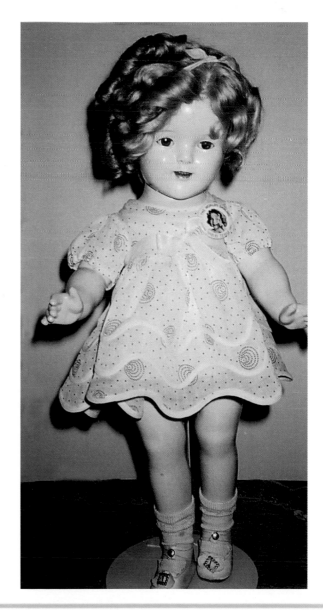

18in (46cm) Ideal Shirley Temple composition doll wearing a rare pink dress with black sea scallop pattern from the film *Stand Up & Cheer*.
$1400
(Loretta McKenzie)

Above:
16in (41cm) Ideal Shirley Temple composition doll wearing a floral pink and yellow version of the dress from *Stand Up & Cheer*.
$1600-$1800
(Loretta McKenzie)

Left:
22in (56cm) Shirley Temple doll wearing a white, knife-pleated dress with tiny red polka dots and authentic fur coat and hat. All-original and fully tagged. Excellent condition.
Doll $2400
Fur Coat/Hat $300
(Loretta McKenzie)

18in (46cm) Ideal Shirley Temple composition doll wearing an original black velvet coat and hat with white cording trim.
$1400 - $1600
(Loretta McKenzie)

18in (46cm) Ideal Shirley Temple composition doll wearing a white corduroy coat and hat from the final scene of the film *Bright Eyes*. All-original and fully marked with the woven NRA tag inside.
$1500
(Loretta McKenzie)

18in (46cm) Ideal Shirley Temple composition doll wearing a rare yellow and plaid coat and hat. All-original and fully marked with woven NRA tag inside.
$2000
(Loretta McKenzie)

18in (46cm) Composition doll wearing black velvet coat and hat, made as an exact replica of the outfit given to her as a gift for being inducted into the "American Legion" of which Shirley Temple was an honorary member. All-original.
$1600
(Loretta McKenzie)

18in (46cm) Ideal Shirley Temple composition doll wearing a rare floral version of *Heidi*. This doll is from the "make up" period and has excellent facial coloring and original wig set.
$1500-$1700
(Tonya Bevardi)

22in(56cm) Beautiful "make up" period composition Shirley wearing unusual aqua blue dress with braided rainbow trim. All-original.
$1400
(Rita Dubas)

Ideal Shirley Temple composition doll wearing a red zipper dress with white leaf trim. This is a hard-to-find outfit from the film *Little Miss Broadway*. All-original.
$1500 - $1600
(Loretta McKenzie)

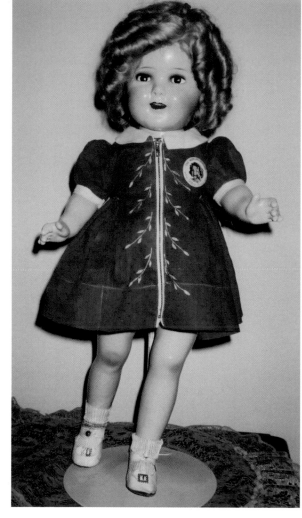

18in (46cm) Ideal Shirley Temple composition doll wearing a rare dress from the film *The Littlest Rebel*. Replaced hat and in excellent condition.
$1800-$2000
(Loretta McKenzie)

Ideal Shirley Temple wearing a
common *Stand Up & Cheer* dress.
All-original and in excellent condition.
$1200
(Bernice Arborlay)

1937 22in (56cm) Ideal Shirley Temple doll
wearing an extremely rare pink traveling suit
from the film *Wee Willie Winkie*. This suit
also came in blue or green. These costumes
were made in moderation due to the decline
in popularity of Shirley's movies and dolls.
$2400-$2500
(Tonya Bevardi)

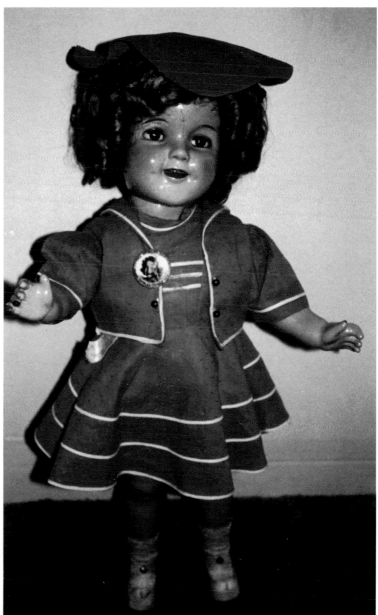

20in (51cm) Ideal Shirley Temple doll wearing an unusual coral dress with rainbow trim from the film *Stowaway*.
$2000-$2200
(Loretta McKenzie)

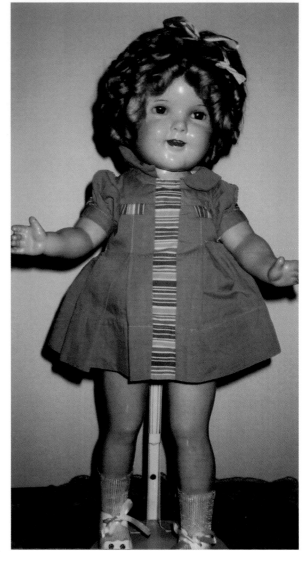

27in (69cm) Ideal Shirley Temple composition doll wearing an original powder blue Nannette dress shown here with the original dress package.
$2500-$2700
(Loretta Beilstein)

Ideal Shirley Temple composition doll wearing a blue floral dress with white apron from the film *The Littlest Rebel* marked Ideal SHIRLEY TEMPLE.
$1600
(Loretta McKenzie)

18in (46cm) Ideal Shirley Temple doll wearing a rare white, yellow, light and dark blue box pattern dress possibly a department store special.
$1200-$1300
(Loretta McKenzie)

Ideal Shirley Temple doll wearing a common pink cotton organdy dress from the film *Curly Top*. These dresses also came in white, green, blue and yellow. Satin ribbons were sewn into the sides to tie to the doll's wrists to give the flaring out effect for which Shirley Temple was famous. From the "make up" period. All-original.
$1400
(Loretta McKenzie)

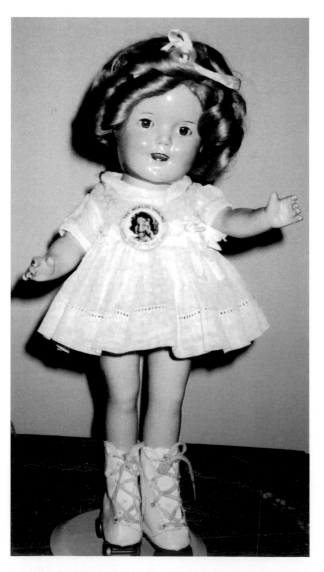

Ideal Shirley Temple doll wearing white cotton dress with a cherry on the shoulder and a pair of period "Sonja Hennie" roller skates.
$1500
(Loretta McKenzie)

Ideal Shirley Temple composition
doll wearing a rare pink, blue and
white boxed-pattern dress. This doll
has a more grown-up hairstyle and
is in excellent condition.
$1500
(Rita Dubas)

1935 Ideal Shirley Temple composition doll
wearing a yellow and blue cotton dress
with braided appliqué on the bodice.
All-original and in excellent condition.
$1300
(Rita Dubs)

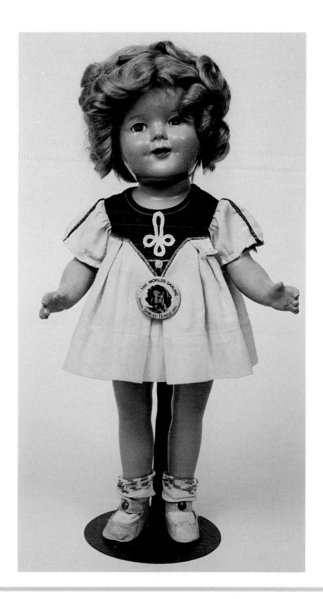

1935 Ideal Shirley Temple composition doll wearing an all-original white anchor dress from the film *Poor Little Rich Girl.* Shirley has many publicity photos wearing similar dresses that also came in navy blue with red trim and green and white with floral trim.
$1300
(Rita Dubas)

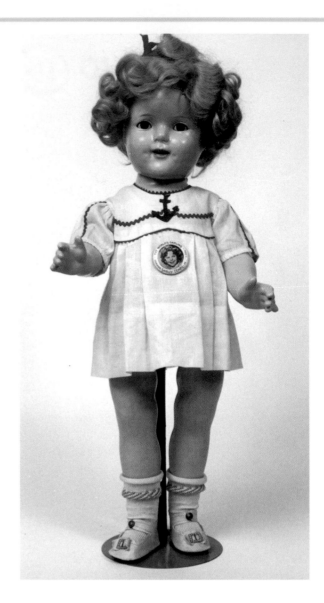

1935 Ideal Shirley Temple composition doll wearing a taffeta and velvet dress with floral (or duck) appliqués on them from the film *Curly Top.* All-original and fully tagged.
$2000
(Loretta McKenzie)

27in (69cm) Ideal flirty-eyed Shirley Temple composition doll wearing a stunning version of the "Texas Ranger" outfit. Excellent condition, missing gun belt and holster. This costume originally came with a ten-gallon hat, cotton bolero shirt, real leather vest and chaps, gun and holster, leatherette shoes and a matching hatband that would read "RIDE EM COWBOY". This costume was a remake of her outfit worn to celebrate the Texas Centennial in 1936. Doll in costume **$3000**
(Richard and Joan Kaaihue)

27in (69cm) Ideal Shirley Temple doll wearing her original yellow and royal blue silk pajamas from the film *Stowaway*. This is a rather uncommon outfit and very few were manufactured.
$3000
(Loretta McKenzie)

Still in her original box, this Shirley Temple doll is wearing a red Scotty dress seen in many of her 1935 promotional photos. It also came in blue and white.
$1800
(Loretta McKenzie)

17in (43cm) Shirley Temple composition doll wearing a navy blue sailor suit seen in the film *Captain January*. This costume came in the following variations: White shirt with white pants, navy shirt with white pants, and white shirt with powder blue pants. It typically had red buttons and a tie around the neck. On occasion, there have been dolls with anchor appliqués on them, and the dolls came with a blue or white navy cap. This doll has a lovely full wig, excellent facial coloring and a replaced neck tie.
$1500
(Loretta McKenzie)

*Note—A 27in(69cm) mint condition Ideal Shirley Temple doll in an all white sailor suit sold for $3700 at auction in 1998.

1935 22in (56CM) Ideal Shirley Temple composition doll wearing a white version of the dress from the film *The Little Colonel*. These elaborate dresses were sold in powder blue, pale pink, cotton candy pink, and yellow. They often had embroidered pantaloons with lace trim, and fancy brow bonnets with feathers or flowers on it. Collectors consider this the most sought after costume, and it usually commands top dollar at auction.
$3500
(Richard and Joan Kaaihue)

Copies of three original Shirley Temple composition doll advertisements from the Sears catalogue ©1935-1939.

PHOTOGRAPH

"I Sleep"
"I have Real Lashes.."
"I Stand Alone"

$2.89 13-In. Size

The Only Original
SHIRLEY TEMPLE Doll
Sold by Mail Only by Sears

LOOK, it's Shirley! Adorable Shirley Temple with golden blonde ringlets all over her head; lovely hazel, unbreakable eyes with real lashes; Shirley's cute chubby face and famous cute dimples around her mouth. And dressed in the same coin dot organdy dress and ribbon hair bow, rayon socks and white buckled shoes and dainty underthings that Shirley wore in her first picture! **And a Shirley Temple badge and silk label on her dress to show she's the only genuine Shirley Temple!**

The Nation's Sweetheart

There isn't a little girl in the world who doesn't want a Shirley Temple doll. She's all of **hard-to-break composition with turning, tilting swivel head;** arms and legs are inside jointed, the better way. Her smiling mouth shows her tongue and teeth. She'll make her new mamma so proud and happy! And she'll bring a 32-page, "Movie of Me," Shirley Temple "book movie" with her. For extra authentic Shirley Temple dresses, see below.

13 In. Tall	16 In. Tall	18 In. Tall	20 In. Tall
Shpg. wt., 1 lb. 8 oz.	Shpg. wt., 2 lbs. 1 oz.	Shpg. wt., 3 lbs.	Shpg. wt., 3 lbs. 8 oz.
49 K 3297	49 K 3298	49 K 3299	49 K 3296
$2.89	$3.79	$4.79	$5.79

Shirley Temple Party Dress
Authentic style. Pleated pink organdy lace and ribbon trimmed. With undies.
Shipping weight, 8 ounces.
49 K 3596—For 13-in. Doll..$0.94
49 K 3597—For 16-in. Doll. 1.39
49 K 3598—For 18-in. Doll. 1.49
49 K 3599—For 20-in. Doll. $1.59

Shirley Temple Plaid Dress
Authentic style. Gay braid and ribbon trimmed. White undies.
Shipping weight, 8 ounces.
49 K 3592—For 13-in. Doll..$0.94
49 K 3593—For 16-in. Doll. 1.39
49 K 3594—For 18-in. Doll. 1.49
49 K 3595—For 20-in. Doll. 1.59

SHIRLEY TEMPLE as a Baby
Sold by Mail only by Sears

Just like Shirley Temple when she was a baby! Soft, huggable and adorably pretty. Lovely hazel glass-like unbreakable eyes that move when she turns or tilts her head—**and real lashes over them.** So sweet with her dimpled cheeks and her smiling lips showing her little pink tongue and five tiny teeth! **Baby Shirley cries, too.** Kapok stuffed body. **She also has Shirley Temple Badge and silk label on her dress.** Pleated organdy dress and bonnet; lace trimmed, embroidered, shirred and picoted! Rayon socks, tiny bootees, undies—and of course rubber panties. She has hard-to-break composition head and legs with chubby inside jointed rubber arms.

"I Cry.. I Sleep"
"I have Real Lashes"

$2.89 15½ In.

PHOTOGRAPH

15½-In. Tall	18-In. Tall	20-In. Tall
Shpg. wt., 2 lbs. 1 oz.	Shpg. wt., 2 lbs. 9 oz.	Shpg. wt., 3 lbs. 7 oz.
49 K 3191	49 K 3192	49 K 3193
$2.89	$3.79	$4.79

Do your Christmas shopping from Sears catalogs

Loads of Fun!

EVERYTHING ON EASY TERMS   SEE PAGE II

$5.00 SIZE $2.98 18 in.

Save ⅓ on Genuine Shirley Temple Dolls

A special purchase brings to you the famous little star of Hollywood, reproduced in an adorable doll. More beautiful, more chic than ever and at real big savings! Her large, glamorous, unbreakable, glass-like eyes have long, luxurious lashes. Lustrous blond mohair ringlets worn in true Shirley fashion. New, gay, smart dresses come in assorted designs and colors. The one pictured is her SWEETHEART model, trimmed with pretty red braid and red hearts. Lacy undies, white rayon socks, white snap buckle shoes.

She's all composition with inside jointed arms, legs and head, beautifully tinted and sprayed. Dainty dimples, smiling open mouth give her that famous Shirley expression. Complete with autographed photograph.

13 In. Tall	18 In. Tall	22 In. Tall
$3.00 Size	$5.00 Size	$7.50 Size
49 D 3290	49 D 3292	49 D 3295
Shpg. wt., 1 lb. 12 oz.	Shpg. wt., 3 lbs.	Shpg. wt., 4 lbs. 4 oz.
$1.89	$2.98	$4.69

The Only Genuine SHIRLEY TEMPLE Doll!

"I Sleep"
"I have Real Lashes"
"I Stand Alone"

AUTOGRAPHED PHOTO WITH EACH DOLL

32-PAGE BOOK "MOVIE"

THE WORLD'S MOST POPULAR DOLL

Almost ⅓ of all dolls sold in the United States last year were lovable genuine Shirleys

$2.79 13-INCH

Surprised? We're not. When you see how adorably real-looking she has been made by Ideal's master artists in the World's Largest Doll factory—so beautifully dressed—so human—you'll understand why thousands of little girls want her. There are many cheaper priced, poorer quality imitations on the market; but only at Sears can you buy by mail, the genuine, original Shirley Temple doll authorized by Shirley herself.

Why, this doll is so true to life that you almost expect her to smile, speak, or go into a dance just like the real Shirley! Those famous big hazel grey eyes, so lively, so expressive, with long real lashes—the beautiful golden blond ringlets—her wistful smile showing tiny teeth and the world-famous dimples—will capture the coldest heart. What a thrill she'll give some little girl on Christmas morning! To prove she is the real Shirley Temple doll, she'll bring a Shirley Temple badge with her and carry a Shirley Temple label sewn onto her dress. Hard-to-break composition, enameled many times, to give her the natural softness and charming flesh color of the "World's Darling" herself. She'll stand or sit alone, hold out her arms, turn or tilt her head. Her stunning outfit includes dainty pleated organdy dress with punched embroidered collar, set off with silk ribbon rosette and long ribbon streamers; a silk ribbon hairbow; lace trimmed slip and panties; rayon socks and snap; buckle, imitation leather shoes. Shirley Temple "Book Movie" and autographed photo included. (See above).

13-In. Tall	16-In. Tall	18-In. Tall	20-In. Tall
Shpg. wt., 1 lb. 8 oz.	Shpg. wt., 2 lbs.1 oz.	Shpg. wt., 3 lbs.	Shpg. wt., 3 lbs. 8 oz.
49 D 3290	49 D 3291	49 D 3292	49 D 3293
$2.79	$3.79	$4.79	$5.79

Chapter 4

The Vinyl Dolls From the 50's, 60's, 70's & 80's

The Ideal Toy Company produced a different line of Shirley Temple dolls from the late 1950's through the early 1960's. These were vinyl dolls made to be more fashionable and usually came with trendy accessories. In the 1960's, Ideal produced several other dolls like the Shirley Temple and Little Miss Revlon® to compete with Mattel's popular Barbie®. Most of these dolls were given vast wardrobes and colorful accessories to compete with one another. The vinyl dolls came in 5 different sizes: 12in (30cm), 15in (38cm), 17in (43cm), 19in (48cm), 35-36in (90-91cm).

In 1972 and 1973, Ideal commemorated Montgomery Wards 100th Year Anniversary with a Shirley doll and 4 matching movie costumes. (See page 89) These 1972 dolls measured 14in (36cm). In 1983, Ideal created its 12-doll series of Shirley Temple dolls wearing movie costumes. They came in 8in (20cm) and 12in (30cm) sizes. In 1984 and 1985, Ideal produced it's final Shirley Temple series entitled "The Collector's Edition." Each doll was in a purple box with a large photo of Shirley Temple that was supposed to be removed to be framed. (See page 74)

The following are the markings for the vinyl dolls:

1. On the neck: IDEAL DOLL ST-12
   On the back: ST-12-N

2. On the neck: IDEAL DOLL ST-15-V (Sometimes this letter was N, M, I)
   On the back: IDEAL DOLL ST-15

3. On the neck: IDEAL DOLL ST-17-I
   On the back: IDEAL DOLL ST-17

4. On the neck: IDEAL DOLL ST-19
   On the back: IDEAL DOLL ST-19

Shirley Temple is back

Shirley Temple is timeless and ageless. She sang and danced her way across the silver screen and into the hearts of a generation of Americans. Her curls. Her crinolines. Her knee socks and bows. Her smile. All helped to make her the "dimpled darling of the thirties."

Now, after 35 years, the television screen has replaced the silver screen as her stage. It was she who danced with you on Sunnybrook Farm. Showed you what it's like to be the Littlest Rebel. And took you for rides on the Good Ship Lollipop. Now she is back to shower joy and tears on a new generation of young admirers.

That warmth and fun are here again in the new Shirley Temple doll from Ideal. Her head, arms, and legs are moveable to create different poses. Imagine her in her many different roles. Children of today will love her as you did yesterday. Since 1933, we have made a lot of truly wonderful dolls, but Shirley Temple has occupied an extra special place in our hearts. She was our first love. As she was yours. And now she can be your children's. Yes, Shirley Temple is back... for good. IDEAL

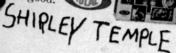

© 1972, IDEAL TOY CORPORATION, 200 FIFTH AVENUE, NEW YORK, N.Y. 10010.

1972 Original ad featuring Stand Up & Cheer

Ideal Shirley Temple 1982 hang tag for 12in (31cm) doll.

All three "Collector's Series" with purple cut out box. (Loretta Beilstein)

Above:
Ranging from 1957 thru 1963, this fabulous collection of 12in (31cm) all vinyl Shirley Temple dolls made by IDEAL are wearing all-original clothes and have many all-original accessories. (Loretta Beilstein)

Right:
1957 12in (31cm) Ideal vinyl Shirley Temple doll wearing a red and white plaid shirt with red shorts and original shoes and socks. She is standing next to an original red-tagged coat.
Doll $175
Coat $75-$95
(Loretta Beilstein)

76

Two 12 in (31cm) vinyl Shirley Temple dolls from 1957. The doll on the left is wearing an all-red version of a sailor suit seen in the film *Captain January*. All-original with her white script purse, shoes and red cap.
$195
The doll on the right is wearing a lovely red floral Bolero party dress all-original and in excellent condition.
$175
(Donna Carr)

Three 12in (31cm) Ideal vinyl Shirley Temple dolls wearing all- original outfits. The doll on the left is in a pink party dress with white rickrack trim. The doll in the middle is wearing the red version of the same dress. The doll on the left is in an insignia skater's outfit with her original ice skates and cap.
Red and pink dolls and dresses **$160**
Ice skaters outfit **$225**
(Donna Carr)

1959 all white sailor suit from
Captain January #9564 complete
with silver script pin and hat
$200
(Loretta Beilstein)

1960 12in (31cm) vinyl Ideal Shirley
wearing a red and white dress with 2
florets in the middle. This doll has her
original box, white script purse, hang tag,
hair bow, and shoes and socks. All-original.
$325-$350
(Donna Carr)

Three 12in (31cm) Ideal Shirley Temple dolls wearing original outfits. The doll on the left is in a 1962 common Shirley Temple style playsuit. The doll in the middle is in her red cotton PJ's The doll on the right is in a pink and white cotton dress with script purse.
Doll/Playsuit $125
Doll/PJ's $145
Doll/Dress $185
(Donna Carr)

Two 12in (31cm) Ideal vinyl Shirley Temple dolls wearing different versions of classic party dresses. The doll on the left is in a powder blue, white and pink nylon dress. The doll on the right is a pale pink and floral dress with original purse, hat shoes and socks.
$300-$325 each
(Donna Carr)

1957 12in (31cm) Shirley Temple
doll wearing a pink floral dress,
complete with original
box and pin.
$250-$300
(Donna Carr)

1957 12in (31cm) Shirley Temple
doll wearing an aqua blue ballerina
costume, complete with original
floral hairpiece and slippers. Replaced
ribbon on slippers, no socks.
$195
(Loretta McKenzie)

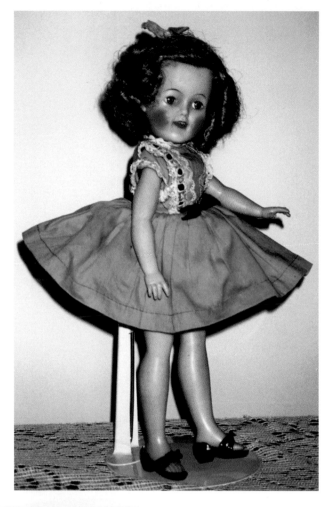

1962 12in (31cm) Ideal vinyl Shirley Temple doll wearing a bright green party dress with lace and black velvet trim. This doll has her original and hard-to-find black plastic sandals and original hair set. Note the excellent facial coloring.
$175-$200
(Vandy Weihn)

Collection of 12in (31cm) vinyl Shirley Temple dolls. Top row left to right: *Rebecca Of Sunny Brook Farm* overalls; green coat; playsuit; and black cowgirl dress. Middle row left to right: red and white *Heidi* outfit; red floral sundress; purple party dress. Front: original white fleece coat with script purse, red dress with white loop trim.
$125-$225 each

Above:
1960 Complete boxed
clothing set #3988. Set
includes a vinyl doll wearing
a pink slip with silver script
pin, taupe coat, matching
purse and woolen hat, a
white sundress with script
purse, a powder blue nylon
party dress, a turquoise blue
pants and shirt set with
straw hat and black plastic
sunglasses.

Side view of the Shirley Temple box with gold stars and label.
$575
(Rita Dubas)

1958 Red, white and blue anchor insignia dress with a matching tam #9506. Dress has small stars and circles imprinted on it, and a petticoat (not shown). Fashion for a 12in (31cm) vinyl Shirley Temple doll.
$95-$125
(Loretta Beilstein)

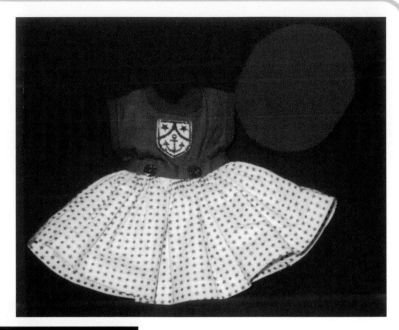

Bolero style party dress of red, white and floral pattern # 9504. These dresses came in a variety of miscellaneous colors and patterns, commonly seen in different shades of blue, green, yellow and pink with floral aprons or sewn on vests. These were originally sold as extra Shirley fashions and were generally not marked. Fashion for a 12in (31cm) doll
$65-$85
(Loretta Bielstein)

Red, yellow and floral party dress possible variation of a Heidi frock.
$65
(Loretta Beilstein)

Common pale pink party
dress with white lace trim.
$65
(Loretta Beilstein)

Common yellow party dress for
a 12in (31cm) vinyl doll.
$65-$75
(Loretta Bielstein)

1958 Light and dark purple
floral dress with lace trim and
silver script pin. Fashion for a
12in (31cm) doll
$85
(Loretta Bielstein)

Powder blue party frock with rows of white lace, flowers and silver script pin. Fashion for a 12in (31cm) doll.
$85-$95
(Loretta Beilstein)

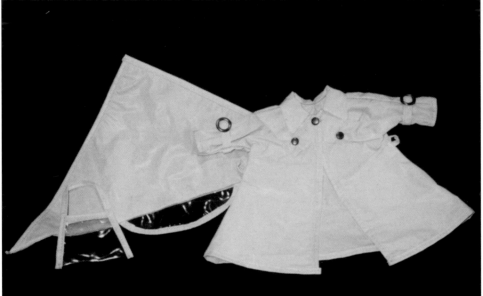

Original Shirley Temple white raincoat with rain bonnet and clear tote bag #9540. Also came in black, red, yellow, and taupe. These were originally sold as part of a boxed set. Out of the box **$75-$85**; boxed and in excellent condition **$150-$165**
(Loretta Beilstein)

Common yellow sundress with blue floral trim. Fashion for a 12in (31cm) doll. These were also commonly seen in red, pink, navy blue, aqua blue, green and white, with any number of miscellaneous floral trims and rickrack designs on them.
$55
(Loretta Beilstein)

Red Bolero dress with black and
red striped box pattern #9540.
$55-$65
(Loretta Beilstein)

Common pair of denim overalls with a
red and white shirt, straw hat and silver
script pin from the film *Rebecca of
Sunny Brook Farm* #9550.
$100-$125
(Loretta Beilstein)

Boxed Captain January sailor suit set. Navy blue shirt, white pants with a red stripe, red necktie, shoes and socks and a matching white hat.
$150
(Donna Carr)

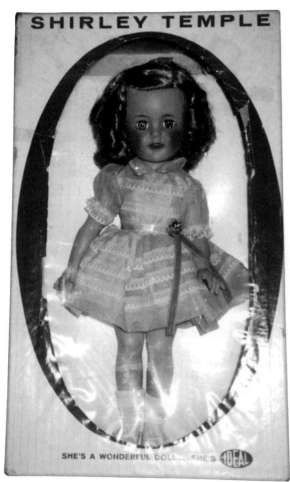

15in (38cm) Boxed vinyl Shirley Temple doll in a pink and white party dress, powder blue felt bow and original shoes and socks. The box reads, "Shirley Temple, she's a wonderful doll, she's IDEAL." Marked ST-15-N
$325
(Donna Carr)

Above:
1961 Set of four 15in (38cm) vinyl Shirley Temple dolls
portraying storybook characters Red Riding Hood, Little
Bo-Peep, Cinderella and Alice In Wonderland. Marked ST-
15-N, each doll came with a wrist hangtag and a silver
script pin. Excellent condition, marked ST-15-N.
$350 each
(Loretta McKenzie)

Right:
1960 15in (38cm) vinyl Shirley Temple doll wearing taupe
jacket and red plaid skirt, a matching hat with original
shoes and socks from the film Wee Willie Winkie #9560.
All-original and fully-tagged. Marked ST-15-N.
$375
(Loretta Beilstein)

1960 15in (38cm) Boxed vinyl Shirley
Temple doll wearing a powder blue
dress with white lace and black velvet
trim, excellent condition.
$325-$375
(Loretta McKenzie)

1959 15in (38cm) Ideal Shirley Temple vinyl
doll marked ST-15-N. All-original white nylon
dress with lace trim, shoes and socks.
$175
(Patricia LeGrand)

1972-73 15in (38cm) Ideal vinyl and plastic Shirley Temple doll wearing a red, white, and floral pattern dress. This doll was one of Montgomery Wards "Yesterday's Darling" dolls that also came in a red and white dress.
$225-$250
(Loretta Beilstein)

17in (43cm) and 15in (38cm) Ideal vinyl Shirley Temple dolls in different Heidi costumes. All-original and complete with their hard-to-find black velvet hats.
Doll 17in (43cm) $350-$400
Doll 15in (38cm) $275-$300
(Donna Carr)

Three vinyl Shirley Temple dolls wearing similar versions of the popular Heidi outfit. The dolls measure left to right: 17in (43cm), 15in (38cm), and 12in (31cm). All-original and in excellent condition.
Doll 17in (43cm) $350-$400
Doll 15in (38cm) $275-$300
Doll 12in (31cm) $195-$225
(Donna Carr)

1960 15in (38cm) Mint-in-the box, Ideal vinyl Shirley Temple doll wearing the black, white and red version of Heidi. The box label reads "Fairyland Heroine Collection". This doll with marked box is rather unusual and very hard to find.
$375-$400
(Loretta McKenzie)

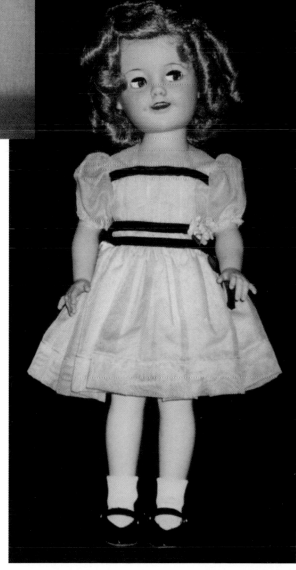

Above:
Two 1957 15in (38cm) Ideal vinyl Shirley Temple dolls. The doll on the left is wearing a baby blue party dress with white lace and a silver script pin. The doll on the right is in a navy blue sailor dress, matching hat and white belt with stars printed on it. All-original and in excellent condition.
$250-$300 each
(Donna Carr)

Right:
17in (43cm) Ideal vinyl Shirley Temple doll with flirty eyes, wearing a common powder blue party dress with black velvet trim. This dress came in many different shades of blue, pink, yellow, green and white, all of which had a velvet trim around the chest and bodice area creating a box or a stripe pattern.
$359-$400
(Donna Carr)

Above:
Two 19in (48cm) Ideal vinyl Shirley Temple dolls from 1958. The doll on the left was the year 2000 Blue-ribbon-winner in Atlanta, Georgia. She is wearing a powder blue dress with a white apron and gold script pin. The doll on the right is boxed and wearing a striped version of the same dress. Both have their original hangtags and are in excellent condition.
$450-$500 each
(Courtesy Donna Carr)

Left:
1960 19in (48cm) Ideal vinyl Shirley Temple doll wearing a pink satin party dress with black velvet trim. The original price tag on the box says "Big Scott's Department Store $9.98."
$450-$500
(Bernard Spinnard)

1960 19in (43cm) Beautiful mint condition Ideal vinyl Shirley Temple doll wearing a rare and hard-to-find orange dress with green and white trim. She is holding an orange script purse, and has an original script pin. Ideal box has majestic horses, lords and ladies printed on it.
$500
(Rita Dubas)

19in (48cm) Ideal vinyl Shirley Temple doll wearing periwinkle velvet-topped floral dress, original hangtag and white purse. These dresses also came in red, green, pink and different shades of blue with floral pattern skirts. Excellent facial coloring. All-original.
$525
(Loretta Beilstein)

1958 19in (48cm) Wonderful vinyl Ideal Shirley Temple doll wearing a red and white poodle dress with silver script pin. All-original and in excellent condition. Marked ST-19-1.
$575
(Loretta Beilstein)

1959 19in (49cm) Ideal vinyl Shirley Temple doll in a pink and white check pattern dress. Black velvet sleeve, script pin and purse. All-original and in excellent condition.
$525
(Loretta Beilstein)

1959 17in (43cm) Ideal flirty-eyed vinyl Shirley Temple doll wearing a common powder blue party frock, complete with tagged dress and original wrist hangtag.
$325
(Loretta Beilstein)

1960 17in (43cm) Ideal vinyl Shirley Temple Ideal doll wearing an original red and black dress, round curlers bag and script pin. All-original and in excellent condition.
$350

1959 17in (43cm) Ideal vinyl Shirley Temple doll wearing a powder blue nylon dress with lace and white nylon apron. All-original and in excellent condition.
$375
(Bernice Arborlay)

1957 17in (cm) Vinyl Shirley Temple wearing a red and white tulip dress with red purse, tag and box. Sleep eyes.
(Donna Carr)

1959-1960 Highly unusual original store display container holding a 19in (48cm) Ideal vinyl Shirley Temple doll with flirty eyes. The label reads "TWINKLE EYE." This doll has her original wrist hangtags, and box of miniature curlers at her feet.
$700
(Rita Dubas)

1960 17in (43cm) Ideal vinyl Shirley Temple doll wearing a pale pink nylon dress with powder blue lace and trims. Fully tagged and in original box. The complete tag reads "The Twinkle Eyes Doll A wash and wear nylon dress" & "An original Shirley Temple Doll"
$600
(Richard and Joan Kaaihue)

1963 17in (43cm) Ideal vinyl Shirley Temple doll in a powder blue dress with black velvet trim and original silver script pin.
$375-$400
(Loretta Beilstein)

Two 19in (48cm) Ideal vinyl Shirley Temple dolls from 1957 and 1959. Each doll has a different wig, face and expression. The doll on the left has slightly different coloring and is wearing an original pair of black nylon gloves (very hard to find). Both are original and in excellent condition.
$450-$500 each
(Rita Dubas)

17in (43cm) and 15in (38cm) vinyl Shirley Temple dolls wearing the same red, white and blue dresses. All-original and in excellent condition. $250-$350 (Loretta Beilstein)

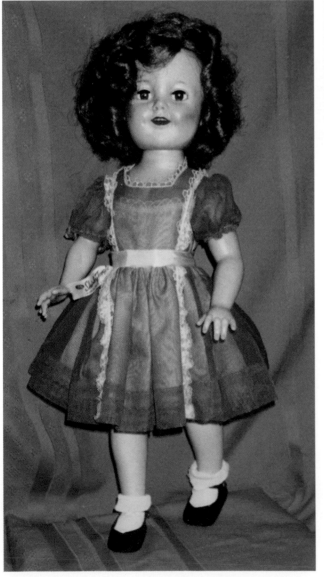

19in (48cm) Ideal vinyl Shirley Temple doll with flirty eyes wearing an original pink party dress with white lace trim. Original shoes and socks. Doll's legs are faded. Marked ST-19-1. $325

Above:
Two 15in (38cm) Ideal vinyl Shirley Temple dolls wearing colorful
floral printed dresses. All-original and in excellent condition.
$275-$325 each
(Donna Carr)

Right:
15in (43cm) Ideal vinyl Shirley Temple doll wearing an adorable
blue jean jumper with red and white plaid shirt and pockets.
$225
(Donna Carr)

19in (48cm) Ideal vinyl Shirley Temple doll wearing a powder blue and pink nylon dress. All-original and in excellent condition.
$525
(Donna Carr)

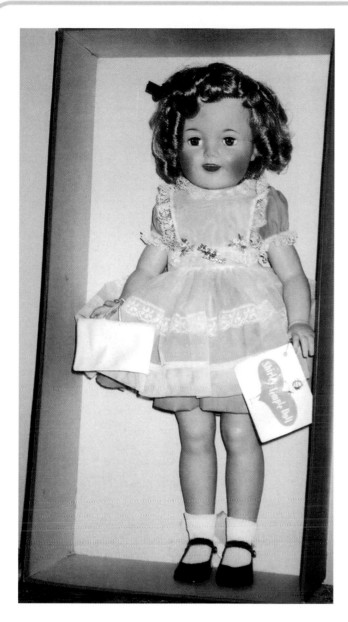

19in (48cm) Ideal vinyl Shirley Temple doll wearing an aqua green dress with a white apron. Complete with original box, tags, script pin and purse.
$550
(Donna Carr)

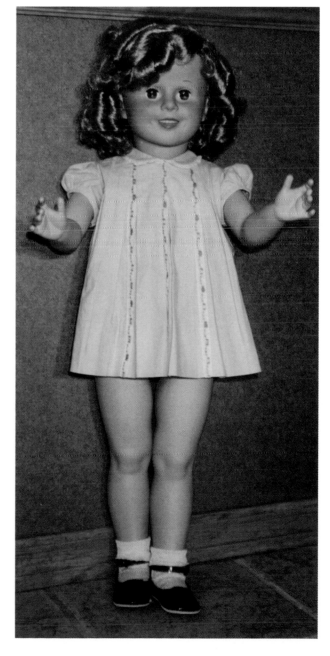

1981-1984 36in (91cm) Dolls, Dreams and Love vinyl doll nicely redressed in an original Nannette dress. $400. Dolls, Dreams & Love dolls came in two sizes: 36in (91cm) and a baby doll in a pink and white gown and bonnet. Dolls, Dreams and Love dolls in original condition
$300
Dresses **$25-$35**
(Donna Carr)

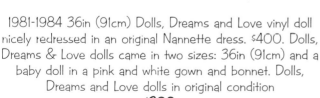

The Official Shirley Temple Black plastic doll was made in 1984 to commemorate the 50th Anniversary of Shirley's films (Came with a large yellow button).

1972 Ideal mint in the box
Shirley Temple doll.
$225-$250

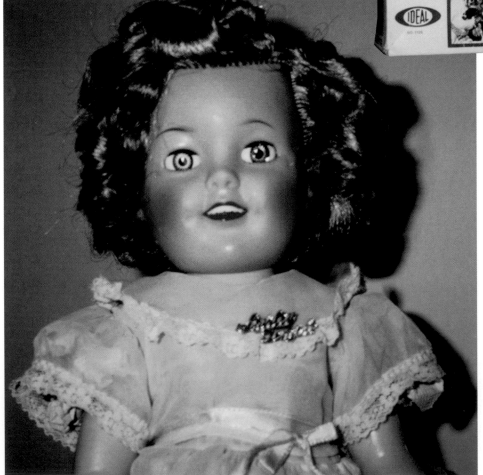

Close up of a 15in (43cm)
Ideal Shirley Temple doll
with excellent facial coloring
and silver script pin.
$225
(Mrs. Mary Whalen)

1998's Blue Ribbon winner at the Atlanta Convention. 19in (48cm) Ideal mint-in-the-box vinyl Shirley Temple doll wearing a baby blue nylon dress with white apron, and original tag.
$600
(Donna Carr)

Rare version of the 1972 *Stand Up & Cheer* vinyl doll wearing the impossible to find red velvet hat, and matching red nylon gloves.
Perfect condition **$300**

Danbury Mint "Dress Up Doll" with two of her outfits. This doll was given away for free with the purchase of the 25-outfit collection sold exclusively by The Danbury Mint. Set came with a large red wardrobe trunk
Doll $75
Dresses separately $25-$45 each
The complete set of doll, wardrobe & clothing $1500 and up.

19in (48cm) and 17in (43cm) Ideal vinyl Shirley Temple dolls all-original and in great condition.
Doll 19in (48cm) $475
Doll 17in (43cm) $375
(Donna Carr)

1960 36 (91cm) Ideal vinyl Shirley Temple doll as *Heidi*. All-original.
$1800
(Donna Carr)

Two 1960 36in (91cm) Ideal vinyl Shirley Temple Play Pal Dolls. The doll on the left is nicely redressed. The doll on the right is all-original. Redressed **$800**; All-original **$1500** (Donna Carr)

*NOTE--A 36in(91cm) perfect Ideal Shirley Temple doll in her original, but damaged box sold for $2025 at a private auction June 2001.

1998's Chicago Blue Ribbon Winner, Original Shirley Temple Play Pal Doll. 36in (91cm)
Ideal vinyl doll in original store bought box.
$2200
(Donna Carr)

Item Not Shown
Shirley Temple script pin silver/gold large for 36in (91cm) doll separately **$35-$45**; untarnished silver/gold
for small dolls **$25-$35**.

Chapter 5

You Name It, They Made It!

Strange, Rare and Foreign Shirley Temple Items

In searching far and wide, I have come to the conclusion that somewhere along the way people were so crazy for Shirley Temple that they made unusual and sometimes very strange items in her likeness. Between the years of 1934 right through today, there are literally hundreds of items ranging from Shirley Temple soda pop to the Shirley Temple Hassock. Why some of these items were actually made may never be fully known, but the avid collectors have found some of the strangest objects to add to their collections.

Very rare 1933 wedding keepsake booklet from the Maltby-Campbell Company of Oswego, New York. It shows Shirley Jane Temple with Gloria Stuart and Anita Louise of the Wampas Baby Stars in a 1933 Bridal Show at Hollywood. Colored photo placed inside the front cover. The owner of this unusual publication was encouraged to preserve the memories of "her day" under such headings as "Gifts and Guests". Measures 6¼-in x 9½-in (15cm x 23cm), $ 350-$400
(Rita Dubas)

Very rare white rabbit muff originally owned by Shirley Temple. This muff was given as a gift to the wife of J. Craig Hille who was the Head of Publicity for M.G.M. He was famous for being "The Artist to The Stars".
Muff $1200
(Loretta Beilstein)

Above:
Amazing contract signed by Shirley Temple,
accompanied by 8in x 10in (20cm x 25cm)
black and white photo.
$5000
(Rita Dubas)

Left:
Fox Film Corporation: final shooting script
dated 10-2-34. This is the original script for
the film *Bright Eyes*. Story by David Butler,
120 pages, **$650-$700**
(Loretta Beilstein)

Above:
Set of three mirrors. The mirror on the left was a publicity photo also made into a mirror. The owner made these items in 1965, but beware of later pieces sold as older models. The mirror in the middle has a photograph from the movie *Heidi* showing Shirley as Marie Antoinette. The Shirley Temple Treasury made the mirror on the right in 1959. Its green band is marked "Japan".
New mirrors $10-$15
Old mirrors $20 and up
(Lorraine Burdick)

Right:
Wooden bowl with wood-burned drawing of Shirley surrounded by grape vines. The outside is surrounded with a geometric design. Signed "Munising" on the underside. 11in (28cm) in diameter.
$200
(Rita Dubas)

Right:
1930's 6in (15cm) wall hanging
Shirley face made of plaster;
unmarked.
$400
(Rita Dubas)

Below:
1935 Rare pair of Shirley
bookends made of chalk
ware/plaster 6¾-in (15cm)
$500
(Rita Dubas)

1950's Children's pink tea set originally came with teapot and lid, cups, saucers, plates, forks, knives, and spoons. Made of a lightweight plastic with tin saucers and plates.
Mint-in-the-box set (not shown)
$300
Each piece separately
$5 to $7 each

1930's Complete child's china tea set shows Shirley pushing a carriage. Very rare.
$400
(Rita Dubas)

Cobalt blue collection.
Large old pitcher $45
Smaller reproduction mug $25
Reproduction shot glass $20
Old bowl $45
Reproduction butter dish $25

Blue items, Reproductions (not shown)
1) "Little Joe" pitcher and drink set with small glasses $75
2) White and blue marble with Shirley picture on it $9
3) Shirley Temple candy dish, also comes in red and green $45
4) Shirley Temple pickle dish $25
5) Salt and Pepper set $45
6) Shirley paper weight $25

New Shirley Temple wall clock
made out of a publicity photo.
$45
(Katelynn Mancuso)

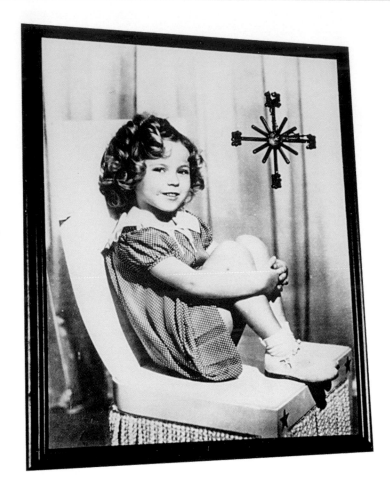

1935 Round Shirley Temple hassock
with airplane photo taken from the
film *Bright Eyes*. Very rare.
$400
(Rita Dubas)

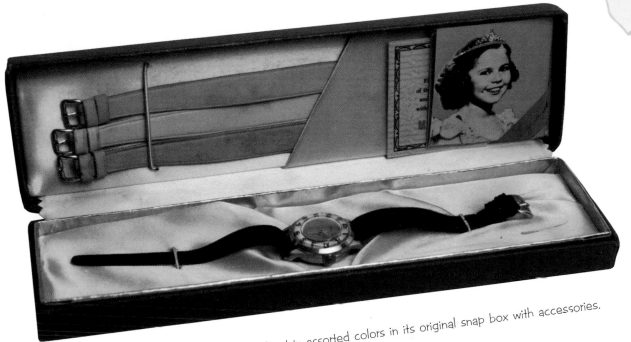

Authentic Shirley Temple watchband set in assorted colors in its original snap box with accessories.
$550
(Rita Dubas)

Y-20- Hand-held child's mirror with photo array (showing 7 pictures) green and silver.
$200
(Rita Dubas)

Right:
1990 Souvenir charm necklace and pin set from the film *The Little Colonel* used as a giveaway gift for the members of the Shirley club.
$50
(Donna Carr)

Below:
1930's Cedar child's dresser holding three photographs:
one-8in x 10in (20cm x 25cm),
two-5in x 7in (13cm x 18cm).
Dresser is 15in high, 20in wide and 7in deep (38cm x 51 cm x 18 cm). Very rare.
$125-$150
(Loretta Beilstein)

Above:
Set of 3 Christmas ornaments designed by Artist
Christopher Radko. Measures 3½-in (8cm) tall.
$40 each
(Donna Carr)

Right:
Unusual 9in (23cm) wooden spindle Shirley doll from Europe;
hand painted features on a wooden spindle disk base.
Extremely rare from the 1930's.
$500
(Rita Dubas)

Left:
16in (41cm) China lamp made by the Goldsheider Company
of Austria. The decorative Shirley figure adhered to the
front is dressed for winter, pulling on her gloves. The lamp
is marked under the brass base. Very rare
$500
(Rita Dubas)

Book *The Boy Who Looked Like Shirley Temple* by Bill Mahan. A story of a child from the 1930's who went in search of fame (biography).
$5

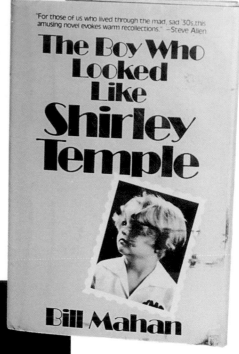

1930's Painted fan with photo of Shirley and her doll on front.
$75
(Donna Carr)

Shirley Temple's delicate book of matches made out of cardboard and paper.
$65
(James Walski)

1937 Very rare all-composition fashion Shirley doll 17in (43cm) from Argentina, marked "Marilu" on back. Fully-tagged dress. $900 (Rita Dubas)

Right:
Hand-carved wooden figure of Shirley in her
first formal gown; marked "Shirley Temple
wears First Long Dress, 11th Birthday Party,
4/23/1940, Made by Holman W. Chaloner."
$700
(Rita Dubas)

Above:
Very rare fully-jointed celluloid Shirley doll from the
1930's. Molded curls painted on copper; measures
8in (20cm); marked "Japan" on a butterfly on the
bottom.
$350-$375
(Rita Dubas)

Right:
Very unusual 1930's chalk ware bust from France
measures 12in (31cm) Marked "Depose 93."
Artist signed F. Coffin.
$450
(Loretta Beilstein)

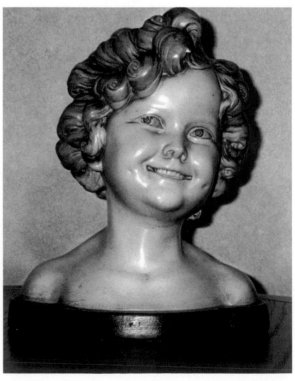

Stand Up & Cheer Shirley soap from 1935. Also came in a "double feature" pack that is harder to come by.
Single $45-$50
Double (not shown) $95-$100
(Loretta Beilstein)

1934 Three different salt figurines measuring 7½-in (18cm) from the film *Baby Take a Bow*.
$50 each
(Donna Carr)

1930's Red and blue metallic figures with removable lids measures 4½-in (10cm) from the film *Baby Take a Bow*.
$75 each
(Donna Carr)

24in (61cm) New bisque Shirley
doll in the pink version of *Baby
Take a Bow*. Hand crafted.
$325
(Nancy Shamberger)

32in (81cm) New bisque
hand-painted Shirley wearing a
very full *Baby Take a Bow* dress.
$400
(Mary Ann Shunk)

TO MY FRIEND.......SHIRLEY TEMPLE

MADE IN USA

Front cover of the Simpco's
ice cream promotional
giveaway photo

Back of Simpco's
ice cream cover

Keep Healthy with

SHIRLEY TEMPLE

and eat

SIMCO'S ICE CREAM

SPECIALTIES

LOOK FOR THE SIMCO TRUCK IN YOUR
NABORHOOD EVERY DAY.

An original 6 pack of Shirley Temple
sparkling cherry soda
$75-$100
(Donna Carr)

Shirley, what big eyes you have! Old
Shirley Temple Japanese fabric fan
Marked Import Da, Japan # 60596.
$75-$100
(Donna Carr)

4 original cans of Shirley Temple
soda pop and root beer ©1980's.
Cans $20 each
(Donna Carr)

Original Shirley Temple ad for "Miss Cynthia's Chocolates," from the film *I'll Be Seeing You*. Very rare
$75-$100
(Rita Dubas)

Metal Shirley Temple cookie cutter along side a sugar cookie shape. In the *Stand Up & Cheer* pose.
Cookie cutter $15-$20
(Donna Carr)

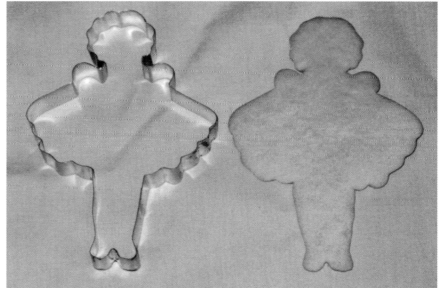

Yellow metal candy tin measures 3-½in (8cm) by 2-½in (6cm).

"The Many Faces Of Shirley" Art Deco style collage of Shirley Temple poster. Created by graphic artist William F. Kraus.
Poster $75
Gift cards $25

Below:
"Shirley Temple The Youngest Monster Sacred to The Cinema of Her Time." This reproduction print was made by Salvador Dali (1904-1989) The Spanish surreal artist who became famous for his classic abstract art designs gave us his version of "America's Sweetheart" in his 1939 gauche, pastel collage of Shirley on a cardboard panel. 30in x 40in (75cm x 100cm.) This hangs in the Boymans-Van-Beuningen Museum of Art in Rotterdam, Germany.
Original work $30,000.00
Prints $25-$35

Above:
"Sidewalk," made in 1983, Created by famed illustrator and artist Andy Warhol (1928-1987). This reproduction screen print is crafted on Dutch etching paper, and signed in pencil. It measures 29in x 42in (74cm x 111cm). The names and handprints of Judy Garland, Jack Nicholson and Cary Grant appear on the print along with Shirley's. Note: Andy Warhol was a big fan of Shirley Temple, and at a recent New York auction, the museum displayed the original 8 x 10 photograph that Shirley signed and sent to him many years ago.
"Sidewalk" is estimated to be worth
$5000
(James Walski collection photographed by Todd Heller)

Left:
1999 Shirley Temple Outsider Art Bottle Cap Pin. Very strange and unusual dancing "Shirley Temple" pin holding a Milagro dolly in her hand. Measures 5in x 2-½in (13cm x 7cm). This piece is crafted out of recycled jewelry, bottle caps, paint beads, small hardware, and a laminated Shirley Temple image face. Created by jewelry artist Ramona Hotel, these pins are unique and one of a kind.
$45-$75

Ashley Rose Orr

The actress who portrayed Shirley Temple in the made-for-TV movie had several items made to promote her. These items were made in limited quantity, and very few were released to the public.

Ashley Rose Orr

Dear Katelynn,
I hear you are a big Shirley Temple fan too!
♡ Love, Ashley Rose Orr

Head Shot of Ashley Rose Orr, given to the author's daughter Katelynn.
Reads-Dear Katelynn, I hear you are a big Shirley Temple fan too! Love Ashley Rose Orr.
$15
(Katelynn Mancuso)

In her first starring role, Ashley Rose Orr portrays the young legendary Shirley Temple, America's original "little sweetheart," who won the hearts of millions as a child actress in the early 1930s. "Child Star: The Shirley Temple Story" airs as a presentation of "The Wonderful World of Disney" on Sunday, May 13 (7:00-9:00 p.m., ET) on the ABC Television Network.

Disney ABC Double publicity photo of Ashley Rose Orr
$10-$12

TV Guide featuring Ashley as Shirley Temple.
$3-$5

ASHLEY ROSE ORR ITEMS (NOT SHOWN)

Ashley/Disney Press Kit containing photo's of the cast & directors. $ 25-$35

Disney *Child Star, The Shirley Temple Story* Starring Ashley Rose Orr as Shirley Temple original movie poster. Very hard to find. $45-$55

Disney promotional photographs of Ashley Rose Orr and cast. $8-$10 each

Too young to read, tie her shoes, or tell time. But by the age of six she was Hollywood's leading lady.

THE WONDERFUL WORLD OF Disney

THE SHIRLEY TEMPLE STORY

How the littlest star in America became the most powerful.

abc 7 PM abc7

disney.com

©Disney

Chapter 6

Restoration and Care
The Composition Doll

The composition doll is made from a porous material that expands and breaks down over time. Composition dolls' clothes are delicate and should be handled with extreme care, and should only be professionally restored.

The Breakdown of A Composition Doll

A) Mohair becomes dusty, uncurled and thin.
   (Please treat with care, gently re-form curls and pin with hairpins)
B) Paint may rub off of the nose, lips, cheeks and eyebrows.
   Find a doll hospital that specializes in facial painting
C) Eye sockets can crack above or below the eye.
   These small cracks can be filled with a wood putty, and lightly repainted.
D) Eyes become cloudy and look dry.
   Use a cotton swab soaked in leather oil and add directly to the eye. This should be repeated several times to achieve a darker appearance. Under no circumstance should you poke the dolls eye with a pin or sharp object, as this may result in the eye crumbling and falling out. Leather oil is safe for both eye and composition. Please repeat several times a year in order to prevent further damage.
E) You can rub Nivea™ lotion on composition; this will moisturize and shine your doll to help retain its original shiny appearance. Most composition dolls will require a moisture rub every few months to retain its appearance and keep the composition from future cracking and crazing.

Two examples of composition Shirley Temple heads prior to restoration. Both are in extremely poor condition.

Rear view of an original composition Shirley Temple doll in poor condition.

134

Before view of Shirley Temple
doll seen on opposite page.
Hair needs to be re-curled.

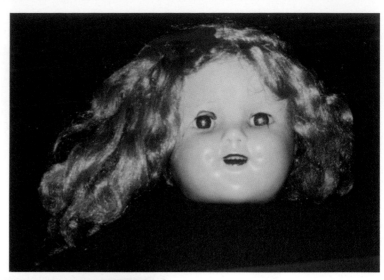

Problems with the doll's arms and legs.

Problems with the Doll's Body

A) Paint may rub off.
B) Cracks may cover the entire body. (Cracks can be filled with wood putty)
C) Seams may split and the doll will have to be repaired professionally.

Problems with the Doll's Arms and Legs.

A) Fingers and toes may break off or chip. They can easily be replaced by a doll doctor.
B) Seams may split.
C) Cracks and crazing may cover the doll's arms and legs. Some cracks and crazing can be touched up; other dolls should be restored and treated by a professional doll hospital.

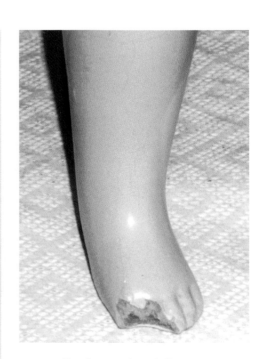

Problems with a doll's feet.

Restored composition doll. Hair was re-curled, and cracks in body were filled and touched up with paint. The doll is wearing a new tailored dress from the film *Stand Up & Cheer* pattern. (Dress courtesy of Cathy Kaufman)

The Vinyl Doll

1972 Shirley Temple doll.
Before vinyl restoration.

Vinly Doll Restoration Tips

Make sure you DO NOT do this to a composition doll!

Steps to a making Shirley look like new:

1) You can wash a VINYL doll's hair with a mild shampoo and conditioner. Unless the doll's hair is dirty, I generally do not wash the 1950's vinyl doll's hair. I usually just try to re-curl with better results.

2) Gently comb through the synthetic hair with a wide comb. In some cases, the curls just need to be gently pinned back into place.

3) Using a photograph or another doll as a guide, try to re-curl the hair into separate curls.

4) To form a new hair style on your Shirley Doll, gently grasp enough hair to form a curl, place a hairpin at the end and slowly roll down towards the scalp. Pin the new curl and move on to the next one.

5) After you have a head of curled hair, follow through and redo the curls again. This time set them tighter and closer together.

6) Repeat the process until you have achieved the desired effect. It takes a lot of practice (I have been doing this for 17 years).

Once Shirley's hair is where you would like it to be, cover the doll's head with a small hairnet (or a homemade tulle net) and spray the hair with a VERY mild hair spray. This is perfectly safe, and will hold the hair in place and give it a new shiny appearance.

1972 Shirley Temple doll before vinyl restoration.

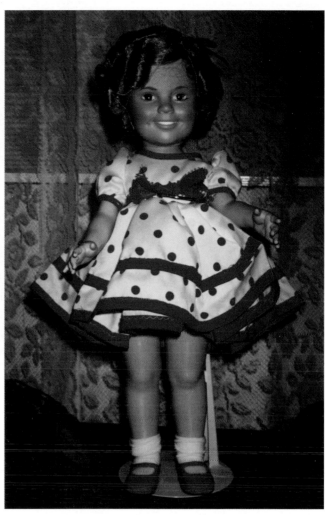

Restored 1972 Shirley doll wearing a
"hand-made" *Stand Up & Cheer* dress.

1972 Broken Limbs Epidemic

The 1972 Ideal dolls were made of a lightweight plastic that sometimes broke over time. There were very few ways to repair these limbs without further destroying the doll. Dollspart Co. has a new line of replacement parts for these dolls. (See Resources section)

Shirley Temple Dresses, Shoes & Socks

New Shirley dresses can be mended if torn, or replaced if they are totally destroyed. And new shoes and socks can be purchased for the dolls. (See Resources section)

Bisque Shirley Temple Dolls

If you have a bisque/porcelain doll with a broken or shattered limb, try to save each and every sliver of bisque for a doll doctor to glue back together. Very often the limb can be saved and mended. You may also choose to contact the original maker of the doll to possibly order a new limb. Sometimes your local ceramics shop can offer replacement parts for new bisque dolls, or they may be able to create a "look alike" limb for the broken one.

Chapter 7

The Shirley Connection

The question many people ask me is where can Shirley Temple items be purchased. The answer is very simple. Shirley items range from antique to modern collectibles and can still be purchased today. Trust me, Shirley Temple is everywhere-you just have to know the right places to look.

BUYING ONLINE

Antique items (pre-1960's) can be purchased at antiques and collectibles shops as well as online. Tag sales, flea markets, estate sales, classified ads, trade shows, Shirley Temple Conventions and private auctions are all great sources to purchase the older Shirley merchandise. Online auctions such as eBay™ and Yahoo™ are excellent sources for both old and new Shirley items. Click onto eBay™ on any given day and there are 900-1400 Shirley items up for auction. There are certain dangers from online auctions. The main risk is that you don't have the item right at your fingertips and therefore you may not know what you are buying. Many auction site give the seller the option to include a photo of the item being sold, but it is still not as good as being able to see or touch the item yourself. I put a big "BUYER BEWARE" on all online auctions.

HOW TO BUY ONLINE

Here are some points you may want to remember for online auctions. Each auction house has its own set of rules and regulations; most of these are followed strictly. If you have signed up for these services, be sure to follow the guidelines properly. They are dealing with millions of people everyday and do not tolerate abuse of their services in any way.

BEFORE YOU BID ONLINE

1) Try to ask the seller as many questions as possible BEFORE bidding on the item!
2) Do not bid if you are unable to ask questions from the seller first.
3) Try to research the item/items before bidding. You may find the seller has NO IDEA what he or she is selling and you may not know what you are buying.
4) NOT WHAT YOU EXPECTED? Try to retract your bid as quickly as possible. If the seller has incorrect information, or you cannot afford what you have bid, explain to the seller and get out fast BEFORE the auction has ended.
5) Do not, under any circumstances, bid on something without seeing a photo of it. You WILL be responsible for payments if you bid under these circumstances. If you choose not to pay, you may receive negative feedback on your "buyers profile," which will reflect poorly upon you.
6) Make sure you read the sellers feedback profile posted. Too many negative feedbacks may mean big trouble for an unsuspecting customer.

Fox Videos with Danbury Mint doll.

7) The most common complaint among the people polled for their opinion of certain online auctions is mainly the drastic rise in Shirley collectibles had driven the cost of dolls and rare items through the roof. People are either paying way too much, or they are having a third party overbid to drive up prices or avoid selling the item altogether.

8) If you pay for something and do not receive the item, contact the seller, contact the auction house and leave appropriate feedback when necessary. Sometimes feedback is your only weapon against a less than honest seller.

9) Postal mix-ups, wrong addresses, incorrect postage, damaged and destroyed boxes-all of these all possible when dealing with shipping and receiving items. Sometimes things just simply go wrong.

Note Most auction sellers are small business owners and private sellers, and for the most part, these sales run smoothly. I do not wish to portray these online auctions poorly. I have had much success finding treasures from cyberspace (online). On the occasion that I experienced a problem, it was rectified quickly. Others lost a lot of money, and did not receive their promised items. Be sure to always bid wisely, and try not to overbid.

Above:
Shirley Temple and Jimmy Durante photo.

Left:
1993 Shirley Temple autograph.

Best Wishes,
Shirley Temple Black
1993

1999 *People Magazine's*
"Where are they now issue."
$5-$8

1999 Though her style today runs toward tailored suits, Black never minded her frilly movie costumes. "They were all authentic to the period," she says. "No zippers, only buttons and buttonholes. But I liked to work, so I'd get dressed as quickly as I could."

1934 Temple's trademark curl on her forehead made its debut in *Stand Up and Cheer.* "I fell and got a bump on my forehead," she says. "My mom put a little curl to cover the bump, and it became part of my look from then on."

1999 *People Magazine's*
"Where are they now issue."
$5-$8

Chapter 8

Resources

I have compiled a list of several businesses that provide the public with current Shirley Temple items. All names presented here are subject to change at any time. You may wish to contact the specific business for product availability and for purchasing details. The author/publisher has no involvement with these businesses whatsoever, and they are to be used as a reference only.

2002 SHIRLEY TEMPLE CONVENTION
September 28, 2002 in Chicago, Illinois

SHIRLEY TEMPLE BOOKS AND REFERENCE GUIDES
The following is a list of Shirley Temple reference guides, books, news, patterns, and other miscellaneous items for researching Shirley Temple dolls and information.

1) *Shirley Temple Dolls & Collectibles* Volume 1& 2, by Patricia Smith (Out of print.) Contains hundreds of color photographs of Shirley Collectibles.
2) *Shirley Temple, An American Princess*, by Ann Edwards. T J. Press, England (Out of print.)
3) *Shirley Temple, Dolls & Fashions*, by Edward Pardella published by Schiffer Publications. Still available, an excellent source of Shirley information. www.schifferbooks.com
4) *Shirley Temple Patterns*, by Sandy Williams published by Hobby House Press. (Out of print.) Authentic Shirley Temple dresses and patterns. www.hobbyhouse.com
5) *15th Blue Book of Dolls Values*, by Jan Foulke published by Hobby House Press. An excellent source of doll information and Shirley Temple doll prices. www.hobbyhouse.com
6) *Child Star: An Autobiography*, by Shirley Temple Black published by Warner Books. (Out of print.)
7) *Shirley Temple Movies*, by Robert Windeller, (Out of Print)
8) *Shirley Temple Paper Items*, by Gen Jones. Wonderful information on Shirley Temple paper items and memorabilia.
9) *Ideal Dolls*, by Judy Izen, published by Collector Books. Contains a large Shirley Temple doll and fashions section. www.collectorbooks.com
10) *Baby-Boomer Dolls*, by Michele Karl published by Portfolio Press. A reference and price guide including Shirley Temple dolls from the 50's. www.portfoliopress.com
11) *The Fox Girls*, by James Robert Parish (Out of print.) This is a wonderful book detailing the life of Shirley Temple and 14 other famous Fox Movie Stars with many photographs and a detailed history.

Shirley Temple

Colorized vintage photo of Shirley all dressed up.
$25-$30

COME JOIN THE CLUB

If you are still craving for more information on Shirley Temple, feel free to contact her MANY fan clubs and news groups for information on Shirley's career, collectibles, dolls and items for sale, conventions around the world, other great fun activities for fans.

FAN CLUBS, DOLL CLUBS & NEWS PUBLICATIONS

The Shirley Temple Collectors News
(Published Quarterly)
(This publication is filled with Shirley Temple EVERYTHING)
Rita Dubas (Editor and Chief)
8811 Colonial Road
Brooklyn, NY 11209
PHONE 1-718-745-7532
FAX1-718-921-6444
Membership/Dues
  USA/Domestic $20 annually
  Canada & Overseas $25
Checks to: Rita Dubas
*VISIT RITA on the web at www.ritadubasdesign.com

Shirley Temple Collectors By the Sea
AKA Lollipop News (Published Monthly)
Members are entitled to Shirley Temple dolls and collectibles appraisals, Shirley Information, convention information, and lots of fun and facts.
Shirley Temple Collectors By the Sea
P.O.Box 6203
Oxnard CA, 93031
Dues/Membership
  USA Domestic $15 annually
  Canada $17
  International/Overseas $ 27
Checks To: Shirley Temple Collectors By the Sea

The Australian Shirley Temple Collectors News
Glen Waverly
55 Botanic Dr.
Victoria 31 South Australia AU
PHONE 0395610238
Membership/Dues
  USA $35 annually
  AUD pa Australia $44

United Federation of Doll Clubs, Inc. (U.F.D.C.)
10920 North Ambassador Dr. Suite 130
Kansas City Missouri 64153
PHONE 1-816-891-7040
On the web at www.ufdc.org
CONTACT (U.F.D.C.) to locate a doll club in your area

SHIRLEY TEMPLE ON THE WEB

• Click on "Shirley Temple" and the world of Shirley Temple will be yours.
• www.shirleytempledolls.com
• www.shirleytemplefans.com (Loretta's Shirley Temple Doll & Info page
• www.shirleytemplefanpage.com
• www.homestead.com/kaa.2000 Joan's Wonderful World of Dolls & Dolls For Sale

SHIRLEY'S ON DISPLAY

Hobby City Doll and Toy Museum
1238 South Beach Blvd.
Anaheim, California 92804
PHONE 714-527-2323
The Hobby City Doll & Toy Museum contains hundreds of dolls and toys, including a large population of Shirley Temple dolls. If you are in the Anaheim area, this is a "must see" for doll and toy collectors.
*Guided Tours, Doll Museum, Doll Hospital, Doll Sales and a wealth of information for your entire doll needs.

Storybook Land
U.S Routes 40/322
Black Horse Pike-Cardiff
Egg Harbor Township, New Jersey 08234
Storybook Land, located 10 miles West of New Jersey's Atlantic City has well over 300 Shirley Temple dolls, figures, collectibles and memorabilia, and hundreds of "Celebrity Dolls" on display in the gift shop. The focal point of the collection is a 1930's composition Shirley Temple doll playing her authentic chord organ.

OTHER SHIRLEY TEMPLE RESOURCES

THE DANBURY MINT
Heirloom Collectibles
47 Richards Blvd.
Norwalk CT 06860-0207
1-800-305-9075
*The Danbury Mint produces Fine Bisque Authorized "Shirley Temple" dolls.

CARON STAMPS
Box 5125
Vacaville, CA 95696-5125 USA
NEW Shirley Temple Stamp Sheets
Patricia Vaillancourt
143 Grand Street
Croton on Hudson NY, 10520
PHONE 1-914-271-5857
FAX 1-914-271-2082
*OLD Antique Dolls & Antique Shirley Temple dolls. Visit Pat on the web by clicking on to www.shirleytempledolls.com LINK

DOVER PUBLICATIONS
31 East Second St.
Minneola NY, 11501
*NEW Shirley Temple Paper Dolls

DEER CREEK PRODUCTION
PHONE 1-954-978-0597
*NEW Shirley Temple Video "The Early Years"

BEAKERS ENTERPRISES
(Monica Sudds Owner)
1-712-642-2200
NEW Personalized Shirley Temple Items
Tote Bags, Address Labels, T-Shirts, Note Cards, Coasters and Mouse pads.

DOLLSPART COMPANY
99 Gold Street
Brooklyn, NY 11201
1-718-326-4587
ALL NEW Shirley Temple items
Shirley Temple clothing patterns, reproduction shoes/socks, dolls clothing/hats
1972 REPLACEMENT PARTS for 16in (41cm) Plastic/vinyl doll

BILLIE NELSON-TYRELL
13035 Ventura Blvd.
Studio City, CA 91604
Antique Shirley Temple Dolls/Celebrity Dolls; write for complete details and updated doll price. COST $5 include SASE

HOBBY HOUSE PRESS
1-800-554-1447
Shirley Temple Doll Patterns/Sandy Williams
Blue Book Of Doll Values/Jan Foulke

CATHY KAUFFMAN
70 Bennet Street
Danville, PA17821
*Reproduction Shirley Temple doll dresses/doll clothes and accessories.
Cost $1 include SASE

TRADITIONS
Home Town Center
Good Hope, CA 92599-4000
A&E Biography on Shirley Temple VHS & Shirley Temple "The Early Years" VHS

NEW VHS FOX SHIRLEY TEMPLE VIDEOS
www.foxvideo.com
Blockbuster Video Stores
Most new video's (Colorized versions) are available where FOX videos are sold

DOLL HOSPITALS
Suzanne Kraus-Mancuso
E-mail address suzannerm1@aol.com (Shirley Temple Dolls Restoration and Care)

HOBBY CITY DOLL MUSEUM & DOLL HOSPITAL SERVICES
(See below for full details)

THE YORKTOWN MUSEUM
1974 Commerce Street
Yorktown Heights, New York 10598
PHONE 1-914-962-2970
Antiques, Toy Trains, Doll Houses, Reference Antiques Library, & much more. Guided Tours and Museum Gift Shop open weekly T-TH-SUN

Shirely Temple typing photo.
$8-$10

Chapter 9

Shirley Temple Facts and Fun

Shirley Temple Facts

1) Shirley Temple had 56 curls, 55 regular sized curls and one spit curl in the front.

2) Fox Studios publicized that she was one year younger than she actually was because they thought she'd be more appealing if she were younger.

3) Shirley was immortalized at Graumann's Chinese Theatre and The Rhodes Theatre when she put her hands and footprints in concrete.

4) Shirley is immortalized as wax figures at three wax museums. Madame Tussaud's in England, The Hollywood and the Movieland Wax museums in California.

5) 7-year-old Shirley Temple was insured with Lloyd's of London. The contract stated no benefits would be paid if the child actress met with death or injury due to intoxication.

6) Shirley Temple made 49 movies in 21 years.

7) Shirley Temple appeared in the book *Ripley's Believe It or Not* for being one of the "Worlds Most Talented Tots."

8) Most of the photographs of Shirley Temple autographed as a child, were in fact actually signed by Gertrude Temple and Shirley's long timed friend and teacher Frances Klampt (Klammie). A true Shirley autograph under the age of 10 is a rarity.

9) In the children's book, *In The Year of the Boar and Jackie Robinson* by Bette Lord, the name Shirley Temple is chosen by a Chinese child who comes to the United States and has to choose an American name.

10) There is a real "Fan Club" for ladies named after Shirley Temple!

Above:
The Yorktown
Museum's collection of
paper dolls, pins,
clothing and large
wigged baby compo.

Right:
Collection of
composition Shirley
Temple dolls,
photographs and
Beanie Babies.
(Lorretta McKenzie)

Collection of porcelain and
bisque Shirley Temple dolls.
(Lorretta Beilstein)

SHIRLEY TEMPLE Beverage
(Courtesy Donna Carr)

8 teaspoons of Grenadine syrup or frozen cranberry
   juice concentrate
1 cup (16 ounces chilled ginger ale)
4 maraschino cherries with stems
4 strips lemon zest
4 Wedges fresh orange

Instructions:
In each of four 6 oz. Cocktail or saucer-style
champagne glasses, spoon 2 teaspoons of grenadine
and fill to the rim with the ginger ale. Stir, and then
drop one cherry and one strip of lemon zest into each
glass. Cut a small slit in the center of each orange
wedge and place on the rim of each glass.
YUMMY!!

A *HEIDI* SUNDAY for kids and grownups
(By Suzanne Kraus)

In a fancy bowl or small soup terrine, place 2
  scoops of vanilla ice cream side by side
Drizzle ice cream tops with cherry chocolate glaze
Garnish with small bits of chocolate around the
  edges of ice cream
Cherry on top
(Alcoholic version) add two teaspoons of cherry
  cordial
Glaze: melt 1 ounce of Hershey's syrup and
  3 teaspoons of cherry juice

The *HEIDI* BURGER with Fries
(originally sold on the children's menu at
Lake Arrowhead Village)

Hamburger
Sesame Seed Bun
Topped with melted Swiss cheese, bacon, lettuce and tomato

SHIRLEY TEMPLE BAR COOKIES
(Courtesy Donna Carr)

Into a large mixing bowl mix two cups of flour
1-½ tsp. baking powder
½ tsp. salt

Mix all together and add:
½ cup white sugar
½ cup brown sugar
½ cup melted butter, stir all together and add:
2 eggs
1 tsp vanilla
¾ cup of milk and mix together and add:
1 cup chopped nuts
1 bag milk chocolate chips (12 oz bag)
One 12 oz jar Maraschino cherries, cut in half, drained

Mix all together and spread in a greased (sprayed)
9 x 13 pan. Bake at 325 degrees for 30 minutes.
Use a toothpick in the middle (if clean) then done.

Glaze: Combine and pour over bars, while still warm
2 cups powdered sugar
2 Tbl milk
½ tsp vanilla
¼ cup butter

ANIMAL CRACKER SOUP
By Jamie Mancuso age 10

2 scoops of vanilla ice cream (Stir until
  half melted and creamy)
Add 1 ounce of mini chocolate morsels
  (Or a candy bar broken into tiny pieces)
Add 10-15 animal crackers
Add a small amount of chopped peanuts,
  or nut of choice
1 cherry on top
Eat and enjoy!

SHIRLEY JELL-O SURPRISE
(Courtesy of the Jell-O Maniac's Manual)

1 box of Cherry Jell-O
Substitute 7 up or lemon lime soda in place of
  the water
(This will become very frothy while being
  cooked)
Follow box directions for chilling
In a fancy small bowl, place enough cool
  whip to cover the bottom of the bowl
Next, layer Jell-O on top of cool whip
Cover the top with a dollop of cool whip
Garnish with cherries and serve

Left:
Collection of composition Shirley dolls,
trunks and wardrobe.
(Tonya Bevardi)

Below:
Collection of all-original Shirleys.
(Richard & Joan Kaaihue)

Prologue

The Slab Story

By Rita Dubas and Arline Roth

Ever met a dealer who has an item so fascinating, so intriguing, so rare, it seems like:
1. It's a once-in-a-lifetime find
2. You're almost certain you've seen something on it before, but you're not quite sure, and the dealer wants more information before he loosens his grip on it
3. It's so unbelievable, it must be phony.

For Arline Roth, both 1 and 2 were true, although for a while, it seemed like 3 might be at least catching up with the others. For this story, we'll need a bit of history and an open mind to digest the year-and-a half long struggle to wrestle the wonderful item to the ground, so to speak.

Let's go way back to 1937. Shirley Temple's cement square at Graumann's Chinese Theater has been dry for two years when a new theater is slated to open in Chicago. It will be called the Rhodes Theater, and is scheduled to open November 19th of said year. But what to do to make it unique? Prints of the stars in the forecourt, a la Graumann's! Squares of cement appear at the studios with the request that the stars press their hands and feet, along with their signature, in them. They will then be sent to 79th Street and Rhodes Avenue in Chicago. Joan Blondell, Carole Lombard, Leslie Howard and Dick Powell are among the stars to get squares. So is Shirley Temple.

The theater opens and operates for several years. It is a streamlined art deco theater. The foyer boasts something like 30 squares set in sand of the stars' hands and footprints. Strangely enough, unlike Graumann's Chinese Theater and Earl Carroll's Theater in Hollywood with its signatures of the stars in cement, not much is made of the display at the Rhodes. The Rhodes goes through many owners; the neighborhood deteriorates but the squares stay. The theater is finally demolished. Hey, where are the squares?

Fast forward to 1991. The Rhodes is long closed. Arline goes to an antique-collectible show and sees a strange cement square attributed to 1930's actress Brenda Marshall on a table. After speaking to the dealer, she finds out that not only does he have 25 squares from "a Chicago theater", but also one with Shirley Temple. Arline silently freaks out and asks the dealer if he will sell it, or if Arline could at least see it. He says he's not sure if he will sell it as he needs more

Slab, still photo of Shirley Temple signing the slab for the Rhode's Theater on November 19, 1937.
(Rita Dubas and Arline Roth)

information on the source of the cement. He's not even sure! Arline, slightly stunned, goes home and calls her friend, Rita Dubas. Arline relates the tale of the cement and asks her friend if she's ever heard of it. Rita, similarly frantic, says no. Both surmise it came from Earl Carroll's theater. Both agree that Arline should not let up on the dealer. Both Arline and Rita start a year-long search for any information on Earl Carroll's or the elusive "Chicago Theater." Arline stays in contact with the dealer and finally sees the cement square at another show. The dealer dangles it in front of her, still asking for info. Arline quotes a price; he considers and refuses to sell it. At that point, the dealer decides he absolutely, positively has to know its source. Arline is heartsick; her husband is disappointed, as he wanted to buy it for Christmas for her.

Meanwhile, Rita is entertaining her husband with the story. Months have passed since the first sighting at the show. Rita has just gotten a book on Graumann's Chinese Theater, partly to search for information on the "Chicago Theater", partly in memory of the now out-of-reach square. It's hopeless. Rita can't find a thing. She's moping. Her husband, in a fit of boredom, looks at the book.

"Hey, Rita," calls the ever aware hubby. "See this picture of Leslie Howard with a cement square from the Rhodes Theater in Chicago?"

In one never-to-be repeated sequence of choreography, Rita swooped down, grabbed the book and dialed Arline. It's early. Rita wakes Arline with the news. Arline gets a photocopy of the page from Rita, calls the Theater Historical Society of America and gets photos of the Rhodes. Pay dirt! She finds a long-forgotten clip in a scrapbook of Shirley signing her square. Eureka! Arline calls the dealer. Success? Not yet.

The dealer has suddenly developed an attachment to the "slab", as it is now known to both Arline and Rita. He says he'll decide on a price in two weeks. He says it will be "closed" to her bid.

A week passes. The dealer calls Arline with a price. What a price! Arline, after months of back and forth, becomes catatonic. She has exactly half of the price he quotes… and she allowed considerably more than her original bid! She calls Rita. They both agree that it seems to be a dead end after so much effort. Neither collector wants to see it go to-who? Michael Jackson? Out of the question. Then, upon the suggestions of Extremely Patient Husbands X and Y, comes a first for either of them-they decide that they will split the cost and share the "slab" between them even though the price was high, it was still much less than if the cement was turned loose in a Hollywood auction. In February, after two weeks and the flu, a jubilant Arline acquires the prize. The plan is for the cement to reside with Arline for a period of time, then Rita for a period of time. Unique, yes, but then so is the cement.

And so, a piece of unknown Hollywood history is safe with Arline and Rita. Perhaps Mel, Arline's husband, put it best in a valentine card to her: "Roses are red, violets are blue, Rita gets concrete and so do you."

Thanks, Arline.

Shirley Temple's Footprints!

Permanently embedded in concrete are Shirley's footprints, handprints and signature.

A still remaining landmark, Graumann's Chinese Theater in Hollywood California, is a very popular tourist attraction.

Photograph of Shirley Temple signing her concrete slab at Graumann's Chinese Theater in California.
$25

Souvenir Postcard "Footprints of the Stars" forecourt of the Chinese Theater bearing Shirley's name and footprints.
$5

Close-up of the Rhode's Theater slab.

GRAUMAN'S
CHINESE THEATRE
HOLLYWOOD

LOVE TO YOU
ALL
SHIRLEY
TEMPLE
3-14-35

THANKS SID
FOR THE HONOUR
Ray Milland

Graumans spoon rest.

ALOHA, Shirley Temple greeting card.
$5

Index

A

America's Sweetheart Collage 7, 128
American Legion, Outfit 58
A Girl Named Shirley Jane 10
A Step In Shirley's Time 18
American Magazine 28
Authentic Autographs 31, 140
Advertisements 70, 71, 73, 123
Argentina, Marilu Doll 121

B

Brochures 22
Box Covers 22, 42, 43
Briefcase, Rare 27
Bisque Dolls 137
Baby Shirley's 141
Buggy, Authentic-Shirley Temple 41
Bolero Outfit, Rare 45
"Bright Eyes" 47, 57, 112, 116
"Baby Take a Bow" 51, 123, 124
Ballerina Doll-vinyl 76
Boxed Set 81
Blue Jean Jumper 101
Bookends 114
Books 120
Bottle Cap Pin 129

C

"Captain January" 11, 13, 35, 54, 69, 76, 77
Composition Dolls 38-76
Composition Dolls Restoration and Care 132
Clothes, Composition Doll Outfits 22, 25, 26, 37
Clock 116
Cinderella 22, 25, 26, 37
Canadian Reliable, Rare 52
"Curly Top" 64, 66
Collectors Series, Ideal 74
Curlers Bag 96, 97
Cobalt Blue Series 115
Charm Bracelet 118
Carriages 39, 40, 41
Celluloid Doll 122
Chalk ware 122
Candy Tin 122
Cookie and Cookie Cutter 127
Chronology 12, 14, 16
Hair Bands 37
Coloring Book 37
"Gold Star" 131
"Gold Star" The Shirley Temple Story 6
Convention News 142

D

"Dimples" 23
Dollar Bill 28
"Dora's Dunking Donuts" Rare 53
Department Store Special 63
Dresses 82-86
Dreams & Love Dolls, Descriptions
Danbury Mint "Dress Up Doll" and
Porcelain Doll Series 16, 106, 116, 139, 149, 160
Hanger, Wooden Rare 118
Dali-Salvador (Artist) 128

Durante, Jimmy (Actor) 140
Dolls Parts Co. 146
Doll Hospitals 146
Dunn, James (Actor) 141

F

Faded Legs-Vinyl Doll 101
Fact Page 148
Fan 120-126
Fan Clubs 144
Foreign Dolls 110
Fur Coat 47, 56

G

Graumanns Chinese Theater 154-157
Giveaway Photo's 15, 17, 37, 39, 142, 145
Gloves 19, 99
Glamour Girl Set 24
Greeting Card 158
Gift Card (Artist) 128

H

Hangers 33
Hang Tag 74, 77
Hair Bow & Band 25
Hair Styler 24
Hassock 116
"Heidi" 59, 89, 90, 107, 113, 145
Heart, Paula & Melissa Joan- (Movie Directors) 16
Hobby City Doll Museum 144
History 12, 14, 16

I

Roller Skates 53, 64
Items Not Shown Pricelist 37
"I'll Be Seeing You" 127

K

"Kiss and Tell" 52
Kraus-William, (Artist) 7, 128

L

"Little Miss Broadway" 60
Lamp, Rare 119

M

Magazine Covers 37
Matches 120
Mask 114
Make Up Kit 24
Make-Up Period 51, 55, 59
McCall's Patterns-Clothing Ad 25
"Mr. Belvedere Goes to College" 33
Mirrors 113, 117
Miss America 34
Movies-Complete List 12, 14, 16
Montgomery Wards –Doll 72, 89
Muff, Rare 111

N

Nannette-Dresses 62, 103
"Now I'll Tell" 45
NRA-Clothing Tags 37, 50, 58

O

"Our Little Girl" 48
Orr-Ashley Rose (Actress) 130-131

P

Patty Play Pal-Doll 107, 108
Paper Dolls 27, 29, 30
Press Kit (Ashley Rose Orr) 131

Poodle Skirt 94
Playsuit 78
"Poor Little Rich Girl" 42, 44, 47, 52, 66
P.J's 78
Promotional Items 29, 33
Posters 26, 32, 34, 35, 36, 128
Postcards 4, 156-157

R

Rare-Photo 21, 110
Radko-Christopher (Artist) 119
Restoration 132
Recipe Page 150
Rhodes Theater 152
Resources/Information 142

S

Sailor Suits 69, 74, 76, 77, 86, 91, 106
Shoes-Leather 20
"Stowaway" 36, 49, 55, 56, 62, 68
"Stand Up & Cheer" 61, 105, 135
Scotty Dress 68
Story Book Doll Series 87
Skater Outfit 76
Sandals-Rare 80
Silver Script Pins 91, 104, 109
Shooting Contract 112
Soda Pop Cans/Bottles 126
Soap 123
"Sidewalk" Andy Warhol 129
Spoon Rest 157
Song Sheets & Music 37
Scrapbook 37
Stamp Sheets 146
Sunglasses-Rare 75, 81

T

"That Hagen Girl" 32
The Little Colonel" 32, 69, 118
"The Little Rebel" 35, 53, 60, 63
"The Little Princess" 49
T.V. Guide 37, 131
Texas Ranger 67
Twinkle Eyes-Dolls 97, 98
Trunks 46
Tea Sets & Accessories 115
The Slab Story 152
Tobacco Cards Price List 37

V

Velvet Coat and Hat 57,58
Vinyl Dolls 72-109, 136
Video's 139, 146

W

Warhol-Andy (Artist) 129
Watchband 117
Wedding Keepsake-Rare 111
Where Are They Now? People Magazine 141
Wooden Spindle Doll 119
Wood Carving Bowl 113
"Wee Willie Winkie" 9, 20, 61, 87
Wigged Baby Shirley 40

Y

Yorktown Museum 146, 149

About the Author

Suzanne lives in Putnam Valley New York, with her daughter Katie age 6, her husband Joseph and his eleven-year-old twins Jamie and Justin. Suzanne volunteers her doll hospital services through The Yorktown Museum, is a member of The Sleepy Hollow Doll Club, The United Federation of Doll Clubs (U.F.D.C.), The Shirley Temple Collectors by the Sea Club, and Shirley Temple Collectors News. She has devoted much of her adult life specializing in the restoration of antique dolls, especially Shirley Temple dolls.

In 2001, Suzanne appeared in Westchester Women's News collaborating on antique dolls and Shirley Temple collecting, as well as winning a blue ribbon on doll restoration from one of her doll clubs. Currently she hosts free doll and teddy bear restoration demonstrations, and teaches doll crafti for children and seniors for m organizations in her area.

Suzanne Kraus-Mancus also the author of several child books "Goodnight, Justin" an The Adventures of Trave Shirley".